T0058129

ACTIVE LESSONS
FOR ACTIVE BRAINS

ACTIVE LESSONS
FOR ACTIVE BRAINS

TEACHING BOYS
AND OTHER
EXPERIENTIAL
LEARNERS,
GRADES 3–10

ABIGAIL NORFLEET JAMES
SANDRA BOYD ALLISON
CAITLIN ZIMMERMAN McKENZIE

Skyhorse Publishing

Acquisitions Editor: Carol Chambers Collins
Editorial Assistant: Sarah Bartlett
Permissions Editor: Adele Hutchinson
Production Editor: Jane Haenel
Copy Editor: Alan Cook
Typesetter: C&M Digitals (P) Ltd.
Proofreader: Carole Quandt
Cover Designer: Scott Van Atta

Copyright © 2011 by Corwin Press
First Skyhorse Publishing Edition 2012

All Rights Reserved. No part of this book may be reproduced in any manner without the express written consent of the publisher, except in the case of brief excerpts in critical reviews or articles. All inquiries should be addressed to Skyhorse Publishing, 307 West 36th Street, 11th Floor, New York, NY 10018.

Skyhorse Publishing books may be purchased in bulk at special discounts for sales promotion, corporate gifts, fund-raising, or educational purposes. Special editions can also be created to specifications. For details, contact the Special Sales Department, Skyhorse Publishing, 307 West 36th Street, 11th Floor, New York, NY 10018 or info@skyhorsepublishing.com.

Skyhorse® and Skyhorse Publishing® are registered trademarks of Skyhorse Publishing, Inc.®, a Delaware corporation.

Visit our website at www.skyhorsepublishing.com.

10 9 8 7 6 5 4 3 2 1

Library of Congress Cataloging-in-Publication Data is available on file.

ISBN: 978-1-62873-766-0

Printed in China

Contents

Acknowledgments

Every book is a result of the input of many people, and a book that is coauthored has more than most. This book arose from conversations the three of us have had over the years. We have each been asked for examples of the active lessons that we use and finally decided that the best thing was for us to write them down.

Sherwood Githens was a professor of education at Duke University and a great proponent of active learning. He passed that love and a great many techniques on to his students. Some of the lessons in the science portion were inspired by his thinking and approach to teaching science.

Elizabeth Birdsong Taylor, a gifted teacher in her own right, was willing to be the guinea pig and read the lessons for clarity. Her comments were helpful in making sure that someone who has no previous knowledge of the information could understand the directions and what the students were to do.

Jacquelyn P. Graham, a teacher at Hannah-Pamplico Elementary Middle School, supplied the idea for Superbowl Writers. Danielle Heffron, a teacher at A. Scott Crossfield Elementary School, developed the Reading Bingo and Bookmarks strategies. Sandy Lorick, a teacher at Langston Charter Middle School, developed the Four-Square Strategy. These fantastic teachers have allowed us to include their ideas in this collection. Thanks also to Andrea Byrns for the map used in Blackbeard's Challenge.

Two of us teach in South Carolina and we are very grateful for all of the support that we have received for our efforts in teaching boys and girls. Randall Gary and Charlene Herring of Richland District Two were instrumental in helping start single-gender education in South Carolina. David Chadwell, the coordinator for single-gender education for South Carolina, is responsible for this book because he introduced the three of us. There are many successful single-gender programs in that state, and if you want to know how to start such a program, his book is a wonderful resource. We would like to thank the students of TWO Academies at Dent Middle School in Columbia, South Carolina, for trying and fine-tuning our lessons. More importantly, we would like to thank those students for being adventuresome and fearless as we navigated through the unfamiliar terrain of best-practice strategies in a single-gender setting.

When you have never been inside a single-gender classroom or seen exactly what teaching strategies are used in single-gender classes, it is very helpful to have access to schools and teachers who have been at this for a long time. Even when you are familiar with this approach, seeing what other teachers do provides a scaffold for expanding your own methods. The teachers in the member schools in the International Boys' Schools Coalition, especially those at The Haverford School and the Woodberry Forest School, have been very welcoming to all of us, sharing what works and what doesn't.

We would like to thank our families: SBA for their help during her shoulder and foot surgery as she worked to produce the lessons, ANJ for their continuing support in her efforts to bring new strategies to teachers, and CZM for their understanding as she tries to teach, get a doctorate, and provide lessons for this workbook.

PUBLISHER'S ACKNOWLEDGMENTS

Skyhorse gratefully acknowledges the contributions of the following reviewers:

Freda Hicks, Associate Principal
Grady Brown Elementary School
Hillsborough, NC

Tasha Holiday, Assistant Head of School
First Presbyterian Day School
Jackson, MS

Donna Lopez, First Grade Teacher and Science Lead Teacher
Rio Vista Elementary School
Anaheim, CA

Eva Myrick, Charter School Coordinator
SLAS-TBP
Dallas, TX

Marci L. Reeves, English Instructor and Mentor Coordinator
Belleville Township High School East
Belleville, IL

Letetia Penn Rodgers, Teacher
St. Thomas, VI

Vicky Ross, Technology Integration Specialist
Kennedy Junior High School and Ranch View Elementary School
Naperville, IL

About the Authors

Abigail Norfleet James taught for many years in single-sex schools and consults on the subject of gendered teaching to school systems, colleges, and universities. Her area of expertise is developmental and educational psychology as applied to the gendered classroom. Prior to obtaining her doctorate from the University of Virginia's Curry School of Education, she taught general science, biology, and psychology in both boys' and girls' schools. Her previous publications include reports of research comparing the educational attitudes of male graduates of coed schools and single-sex schools, research describing the effects of gendered basic skills instruction, and a report of academic achievement of students in single-gender programs. In addition, she has written on differentiated instruction at the elementary school level. She has presented workshops and papers at many educational conferences and works with teachers and parent groups in interpreting the world of gendered education. Her professional affiliations include the American Educational Research Association, the American Psychological Association, the Association for Supervision and Curriculum Development, the Coalition of Schools Educating Boys of Color, the Gender and Education Association, the International Boys' Schools Coalition, and the National Association for Single-Sex Public Education (Advisory Board member).

Sandra Boyd Allison is an experienced educator with thirty-five years of teaching and consulting experience in curriculum instruction, secondary mathematics, and special education. She has presented at local, state, and international conferences and workshops. Her experience includes teaching positions in regular education in grades K–12 as well as in single-gender magnets programs, regular education classrooms, self-contained, resource and itinerant programs for hearing-impaired students, programs for learning-disabled students, and programs for mentally handicapped students. In addition to state certifications in secondary mathematics, elementary education, in teaching the hearing impaired, the gifted and talented, students with learning disabilities, and the mentally handicapped, she has been recognized by her peers as Teacher of the Year and is certified by the National Board for Professional Teaching Standards in Adolescence and Young Adulthood Mathematics. Allison received an undergraduate degree in elementary and special education from Winthrop University and a graduate degree in curriculum and instruction (math and science) from the University of North Carolina at Greensboro. She has received local, state, and national grants from the South Carolina Department of Education, Metropolitan Life Insurance Company, and Time Warner Cable. Allison's expertise is in the implementation of innovative programs that are built around current models of instruction containing core lessons based on state standards. She is a collaborator with a special interest in creating cross-curricular, real-world lessons that combine her knowledge of mathematics with her lifelong interest in science, technology, the history of the United States, and the ancient works of the great thinkers.

 **Caitlin Zimmerman McKenzie** is a teacher of language arts in single-gender middle schools. She obtained her master's degree in education with a specialization in language and literacy and is a doctoral candidate in curriculum studies at the University of South Carolina. She is a consultant in best-practice strategies for teachers in single-gender classrooms.

She has presented at national and regional conferences on teaching language arts in single-gender classrooms.

Introduction

It is now generally agreed that traditional educational methods may not be the best way for all students to learn. School focuses on verbal and auditory skills, whereas many boys and some girls learn better using iconic and kinesthetic skills. What that statement means is that students are generally asked to read about or listen to information as their primary method of acquiring knowledge. But active learners do not learn well that way and are more likely to be successful if the information is presented to them in graphic form or if they are allowed to manipulate materials as part of the learning process. Traditionally, school presents lessons as verbal or auditory information. When active learners are not successful using these methods, they may be seen as having learning disabilities when, in fact, they are very good learners as long as they use methods which are not primarily verbal or auditory. In this work you will find active approaches to math, language arts, and science.

One of the hardest things for active learners to do in school is review. They have already covered the material once: Why go over it again? More important, review is rarely hands-on, but rather involves rereading the material or listening to someone, either teacher or fellow student, verbalize the material. Without some way to get physically involved in the review process, many students find it difficult to pay attention during a review session. You will find that many of the strategies in this workbook are specifically designed for active review. We think that you will find that using some of these methods will increase students' engagement in the lesson and improve recall of information.

This set of lessons was prepared by three teachers with expertise in math, language arts, and science. The math expert is a veteran teacher whose experience is in teaching math and social studies in public coed and single-sex schools. The language arts expert has been very successful in teaching boys in a public single-sex school and is passionate about getting boys interested in reading. The science and learning style expert has taught math and science in boys' and girls' schools over a long career. All of the suggestions in this work have been used in the classroom by one of the three. Bear in mind that these are suggestions, and while they have worked for us and for others we know, they are not prescriptions. We suggest that you use the following lessons as a starting place; we hope you find that they help you develop lessons that work well for you.

What follows in Chapter 1 is a very brief summary of how cognitive gender differences may affect the way that boys and girls learn. The premise of this work is that more active approaches to instruction help experiential learners acquire information and stay focused on the task at hand. If this is information you are already familiar with, feel free to skip this chapter and move directly to the activities. You will find after Chapter 1 a chart (Table 1.1) which outlines how each activity meets cognitive differences directly enhanced by active learning. This may be sufficient to satisfy your curiosity. If, however, this is a topic on which you would like more detailed, in-depth information, you may want to consult the companion books also published by Corwin: *Teaching the Male Brain: How Boys Think, Feel, and Learn in School* and *Teaching the Female Brain: How Girls Learn Math and Science.* These earlier books provide complete descriptions of all of the neurocognitive bases for why these lessons work with students who learn best through iconic or kinesthetic methods. In this book, you will see examples of how others have successfully put this research to use in the classroom, and learn how to apply it yourself.

Each lesson begins with a suggested grade level for students who will benefit from the activity. These suggestions are purposefully vague because students and classes vary a great deal. Lessons for younger students will work with students in Grades 3 through 6 to 8. Lessons for older students are designed for students in Grades 6 to 8 through 10. When the lesson is described as being for all levels, that means that you can apply the ideas to material for your own students, whether they are third graders, tenth graders, or somewhere in between. Some of the math and science lessons are designed for students who have reached a certain skill level, such as lessons for algebra students; but whether your students are in a seventh-grade algebra class or one in ninth grade, the lesson should work for them. In short, not all of these lessons will work for all students in Grades 3 through 10, but you should feel free to adapt these lessons to your class. They have been designed with flexibility in mind.

1

A Brief Look at Experiential Learners

Let us begin by saying that the students who will benefit most from the lessons in this book may be either male or female. They are the experiential learners in your classroom, the ones who need to interact with information in an active way and probably in more than one way. These students are more likely to be boys, for the reasons outlined in this chapter, but many girls are also experiential learners and will respond similarly to the iconic or kinesthetic methods underlying the lessons in this book.

THE ACTIVE BRAIN: MALE OR FEMALE

There is a growing body of evidence that reveals that the brains of very young girls and boys are different—both structurally and developmentally. When we say that boys and girls differ, we mean that the average girl and the average boy are different, but some girls learn more like a typical boy and some boys learn more like a typical girl. Characteristic sex indicators such as hormonal levels do not show absolute differences, although average levels of hormones are very different between men and women (Kimura, 2004). That means that individual men may have the same levels of hormones as do individual women, but for most people, hormonal level is a clear indicator of sex differences. Individuals who are genetically female or male may show variations in the expression of typical sexual markers. For example, although all of the authors of this book are women, one of us is as tall as the average male. That does not make her male, just taller than the average female. So, while we refer to the male or female brain, please remember that we are referring to behavior or responses which are typical for the majority of males or females, but certainly not for all.

One of the authors has been asked why she still refers to the boy brain if not all boys fit the description and some girls actually do fit the description. The problem is that male and female brains do not present a simple dichotomy. Some differences are due to biology, such as the differences in the structure of the ear that result in hearing differences and the hemispheric differences in brain development. If boys don't listen to directions is it due to hearing differences or due to their slower acquisition of language because their left hemisphere is a bit slower to develop? It may be that they don't always understand what is said or it may be due to their lack of interest in the subject. Since parents talk to infant boys less often than to infant girls, the problem may be that boys don't have a lot of practice in listening (Whitehead, 2006). The variations in how girls and boys learn begin with differences in brain development, which are shaped by the differences in how children are treated beginning in the minutes following birth, but since the majority of boys fit the model, it makes sense for teachers to think in terms of a gendered approach to the classroom.

All teachers are aware that there are many different avenues to learning and that to group students by any variable means that there will be a wide range of differences. Knowing that, we traditionally group children in school by age. Even though 10-year-old children can vary a great deal, most children in a fifth-grade class are 10 years old. As much as we would like to do so, it is impossible for a teacher to tailor instruction for each individual child in a class. So teachers focus on the most obvious groupings of students, and sex is one way to sort children. Preparing a lesson to include boy-style learners will meet the needs of many of the boys in a class, but not all. Additionally, the academic needs of some girls, especially girls who are experiential learners, will be met by lessons framed for boys.

Having apologized for the fact that children do not fit neatly into sex-defined learning groups, we still maintain that sex-specific lessons and even classes help a great many children. Simply saying that boys are more varied compared to each other than when compared to girls does not mean that the differences between the sexes do not exist. Of course they exist; what we do not want is for children to be limited in their school experience because they belong to one group or another. Providing lessons aimed only for boys or for girls is akin to teaching a sport only by reading a description of how to play the game without seeing how the game is played.

Structural Differences

Male and female brains do not develop in the same way. By the time we become adults, however, the male and the female brain function more similarly than they did when we were infants. The active approach to teaching is based on the belief that helping children use their cognitive strengths to learn will lead them to focus on academic strengths rather than on areas of weakness. If a child does not learn using conventional methods, that does not mean the child cannot learn. It simply means that the child may have greater success using another approach. Those alternative approaches may be based on cognitive gender differences.

Right Versus Left

For boys, the right side of the brain develops early, whereas for girls, the left side of the brain develops first (Shucard & Shucard, 1990). We know that the language center begins in the left portion of the cerebral cortex and believe that is the reason that girls, on average, have stronger verbal skills than do boys as very young children (Halpern, 2000; Kimura, 2000). By age 15, for example, on a test of reading literacy administered in 25 countries, girls outscored boys in every country by a minimum of 15 points (Halpern, 2004). However, by adulthood, there is no difference in verbal intelligence between men and women (Halpern, 2000) even though men and women continue to process words differently (Goldstein et al., 2007). The right side of the brain is believed to be where spatial skills begin development, and that is usually given as the reason that little boys find it easier to throw a ball than little girls. Unfortunately, verbal skills are more valued in school than are spatial skills, particularly in the early years. Teaching boys to use spatial skills to help remember verbal information is one example of how to use cognitive advantages to compensate for cognitive differences. Giving girls practice in developing spatial skills will assist them when they get to upper-level math and science.

Frontal Lobe Development

The prefrontal lobe, the portion of our brain immediately behind our eyebrows, is referred to as the executive decision maker and is responsible for helping us make reasoned decisions and for controlling impulses. This part of the brain begins to mature first in girls, and the slower development in boys may be a contributor to the impulsive behavior which is a hallmark of young males (Giedd et al., 1999). Studying in short bursts will take advantage of this lack of ability to sustain attention and control behavior and give practice in developing concentration skills.

Amygdala and Hippocampus

These nodes deep within in the brain can be found approximately at the points where horizontal lines running backward through the eyes intersect a line connecting the ears. The hippocampus has long been known to be involved in helping us turn short-term memories into long-term memories. The exact function of the amygdala is beginning to be understood; it is thought to be implicated in emotions such as fear and aggression as well as in emotional memory. The term *implicated* means that scientists do not know if the amygdala is the source of these emotions or whether it is simply a mediator or manager of these emotions, but it is involved. Recently, it has been noted that the amygdala enlarges first in boys and the hippocampus first in girls (Giedd, Castellanos, Rajapakse, Vaituzis, & Rapoport, 1997; Yurglen-Todd, Killgore, & Cintron, 2003).

Does that mean that girls have better memories and boys have stronger emotions? There is plentiful evidence that little girls learn words better than little boys; one study reported that 20-month old girls have twice the vocabulary of 20-month old boys (Morisset, Barnard, & Booth, 1995). That is probably due to a combination of factors including the earlier left hemisphere development of the brain combined with the early memory skills. Little boys certainly have the reputation of being loud and obstreperous, and that behavior can be seen as the result of emotions in an individual with poor verbal skills. Helping boys use their considerable energy and framing the material so that it interests them will improve the chances that boys will learn the material.

Additionally, children who are bored in school become disconnected from what happens in the classroom. Only if the lesson provides control, choice, challenge, complexity, and caring can bright students be motivated to engage in the class exercise (Kanevsky & Keighley, 2003). Boredom is a huge problem for boys in school because of enforced inactivity, and any lesson that provides control, choice, challenge, and complexity, together with a teacher who cares, will engage boys in the learning process.

Sensory Differences

Hearing

Most newborns in the United States receive a test for hearing involving a sudden burst of sound that, if the ear is functioning correctly, results in an echo-type reaction detected by a device in the ear canal. The results of this test indicate that the ears of girls are more sensitive than the ears of boys, especially for high frequencies (Cassidy & Ditty, 2001). Other research indicates that girls' ears are more sensitive to soft (low-volume) sounds as well (McFadden, 1998). Additionally, little boys are more likely to suffer inner ear infections (Stenström & Ingvarsson, 1997), which means that while they have an infection what they hear may be muffled and indistinct. So speaking to a little boy in a high, soft voice may not get his attention or result in his remembering what has been said. Classroom exercises which help boys develop phonemic awareness will assist boys in learning to read and to listen to others. Additionally, training in listening and developing skills in accurately reporting what is heard will help students develop the auditory proficiency necessary to learn in the classroom.

Vision

One of the major problems with vision is *saccades*. The reader will find a complete description of the subject in Chapter 3. Saccades may be larger in novice readers and boys, and an active approach to learning may well get the student engaged in a task; as students gain more control of their bodies, they will be ready to read. Probably related to this situation is the understanding that girls are better at perceptual speed than boys (Kimura, 2000). This is the skill that allows us to locate similar objects in a field of many other objects or determine which figure is different. Proofreading requires good perceptual speed; the fact that many boys will not check their work or are poor proofreaders is probably a result of this gender difference. Teaching boys techniques for finding mistakes will make it more likely that they will check their work and correct their errors.

Touch

While girls may have a greater sensitivity to touch than do boys (Velle, 1987), the observation of teachers is that boys have to physically interact to learn (Reichart & Hawley, 2009; Vallance, 2002). Recent information suggests that boys who are moving, especially moving their hands such as fiddling with something, are better able to remember class information (Rapport et al., 2009). In fact, it is such a salient learning trait for boys that most of the suggestions contained in this workbook are designed at least in part to give students the chance to interact with the classroom environment.

Cognitive Differences

Verbal Skills

It is believed that because of the differential development of the brain, girls have a verbal advantage. It is well established that by third or fourth grade the average girl reads better than the average boy, and that continues to be the case into early high school (Halpern, 2004). The reasons for this difference in performance are complex and beyond the scope of this brief discussion. However some of the factors determining boys' reading achievement have been identified as a perception of reading as a feminine activity, lack of familiarity with books and literacy, weak reading skills, poor academic self-concept, and inefficient learning strategies (Sokal, Katz, Chaszewski, & Wojcik, 2007; Swalander & Taube, 2007). You will note that all of those factors are determined more by society than by biology. The verbal problems that are typical of many boys may start with a neurobiological difference, but are exacerbated by societal assumptions that boys either will have problems reading or don't want to read. Strategies to help boys become more adept with all kinds of verbal skills will help boys feel more comfortable with reading and writing tasks.

Spatial Skills

It is well established that, probably because of the early development of the right cerebral hemisphere, boys have good spatial skills (Shucard & Shucard, 1990). Teaching boys to use charts, graphs, and other graphical methods of organization will help them structure information in such a way so that it is more easily retrieved. The act of displaying words in such a way will help boys remember the material.

Learning Modalities

For whatever reason, boys tend to learn best when they can see the information depicted pictorially—what is known as *iconic learning*—and when they can interact with the information—what is known as *kinesthetic learning*. Information in school is overwhelmingly presented as verbal information or as auditory information. One study of college students found that none of the men in the study preferred to hear about information. Most of the males in this study (87.5%) preferred to receive information in multiple ways, whereas less than half of the women in the study (45.8%) did (Wehrwein, Lujan, & DiCarlo, 2006). When a lesson is designed to help students interact with the information in more than one way, the learning of boys and other experiential learners is enhanced.

LANGUAGE ARTS, MATHEMATICS, SCIENCE, AND STUDY STRATEGIES

The lessons in the following chapters are arranged into four broad areas: language arts, mathematics, science, and study strategies. Many of the lessons in each area can be adapted for use in other areas, and we hope that you will be inspired to develop strategies of your own.

Each lesson is divided into five or six parts: The level of each lesson is followed by the purpose of the lesson, the time required for the lesson, the materials needed (if any), the procedure for the lesson, and suggested ways to assess the success of the lesson. The level will tell you what level of students the lesson is intended for, and also what the lesson is designed to do. Some of the suggestions are designed to teach material and are designated as lessons. Others are for review, to provide enrichment, to help students learn problem solving skills, to provide incentives to learn lessons, or to present information traditionally given in verbal form in an alternative modality. Some lessons are complicated and require several pages to describe, while others are very simple and can be explained in less than a page. Table 1.1 is a chart indicating which lessons are designed to meet specific cognitive needs of experiential learners.

The point of all of these lessons is to provide a more active approach to learning. While most active learners are boys, some girls are also active learners and will benefit from this approach. Remember, too, that students who learn well in less interactive ways will also profit from getting involved in the learning process. All students need a variety of experiences so that they can develop different ways of accessing information. Outside of school, we are rarely handed a book to learn what we need, but have to acquire information by interacting with the environment. These active lessons will help students prepare for the world.

Table 1.1 How the Following Lessons Meet the Cognitive Needs of Experiential Learners

Brain/Cognitive Differences	Lessons to Try			Study Strategies
	Math	Language Arts	Science	
Right Brain Versus Left Brain Allows students with strengths in one side to use those strengths to develop strengths in the other; e.g., helps students with strong spatial skills to help develop verbal skills.	8, 11, 13, 16, 19, 20, 21	28, 34, 37, 43	48, 51, 54, 56, 61	67, 68
Frontal Lobe Development Gives students practice in executive function tasks such as controlling impulses and making reasoned decisions.	3, 5, 7, 10, 13, 14	24, 26, 31, 32, 37, 42, 43, 46	49, 50, 52, 54, 60, 63	64, 66, 67, 68, 69, 70, 71, 73
Amygdala Some students need an emotional connection with a lesson to develop an interest in the subject. These lessons help here.	7, 16, 21	22, 23, 26, 27, 29, 30, 31, 32, 33, 44, 45	48, 54, 55, 59, 62	64, 66, 68, 69, 70, 72, 73
Hippocampus Boys' memory skills tend to be based on visual cues and girls' on verbal cues. These lessons help students develop skills in both areas.	8, 9, 21	23, 32, 39	47, 56, 57, 58	66, 67
Listening If students do not develop good listening skills in part because of different development in sections of the ear, these lessons help develop listening skills.	1, 2, 4, 6	22, 30, 39, 43	51, 52, 53	64, 68, 71, 72, 73
Vision If students are particularly strong in visual skills, these lessons take advantage of those strengths. They also help other students strengthen their ability to use visual cues.	3, 8, 9, 10, 12, 15, 16, 17	25, 28, 38, 42, 44, 45	47, 49, 53, 57, 58, 59, 61, 62	65, 66, 67
Touch Boys report that they learn well from active learning; these lessons provide lots of touch. Girls may be reluctant to engage in such activities and will benefit from the experience.	1, 2, 6, 9, 10, 14, 18, 21	23, 25, 36, 45,	All lessons	65, 66, 67, 68, 73
Verbal Skills For students whose verbal skills are slow to develop, these exercises are designed to provide active and interesting ways to help them practice those skills. Students with strong verbal skills can use their strengths even more.	4, 11, 15	27, 29, 30, 31, 33, 34, 35, 38, 40, 41, 44	55, 60	65, 67, 70, 71
Spatial Skills These exercises will provide practice for students whose spatial skills are slow to develop. At the same time they will allow students with strong spatial skills to shine.	1, 2, 5, 6, 8, 10, 14, 16, 17, 18, 19	25, 34, 36, 40, 41, 42	49, 50, 53, 54, 55, 56, 59, 60, 61, 63	65, 67, 72
Learning Modalities Most lessons are based on verbal/visual or auditory tasks. These lessons provide iconic (picture) and kinesthetic (hands-on) activities.	3, 9, 10, 11, 12, 15, 18	24, 28, 29, 35, 36, 40, 41, 45	48, 52, 53, 55, 57, 58, 60	66, 67, 68, 69, 70

2
MATH

Summer school at the school where one of the authors taught was for students who either needed remedial work or who wanted to get ahead. Consequently, both remedial algebra and fast-track algebra were offered. One afternoon, as she was making her rounds during study time, she came across one of the girls in the fast-track class trying to help one of the boys in the remedial class with some word problems, and it wasn't going well. The advanced student was talking about what she did to solve the problem and then doing it. What the teacher heard as she turned the corner was, "But that is what the teacher is doing in class, and I still don't get it." The teacher asked if she could help and started by teaching the student who was having trouble the technique called Box the Operator. In about five minutes, he was solving all sorts of word problems. The girl in the fast-track class said that she realized that at some level she was using that technique when she solved problems, but she didn't have to mark up the problem. The other student said that this technique worked for him because it allowed him to do something rather than just reading the problem.

This story may surprise you, partially because the good math student is female and the poor math student is male. The stereotype would lead you to believe the students would be reversed, but many girls do very well in math. In fact, on the mathematics portion of the National Assessment of Educational Progress (NAEP), known as the Nation's Report Card, girls score much closer to boys in math than boys score in relation to girls on reading (Geist & King, 2008).

NAEP 2008 Long-Term Assessment

Reading	1980			2008		
	Girls	Boys	Girls/Boys	Girls	Boys	Girls/Boys
Age 9	220	210	10	224	216	8
Age 17	289	282	7	291	280	11
Math	1982			2008		
	Girls	Boys	Girls/Boys	Girls	Boys	Girls/Boys
Age 9	221	217	4	242	243	−1
Age 17	296	301	−5	303	309	−6

Note: Positive score indicates average score for girls higher than average score for boys.

Source: NCES (2009).

In 1982, 9-year-old girls actually scored better than their male age-mates on math, and, while they are now behind the boys, they are making progress. In 1996, 9-year-old girls were four points behind the boys, whereas in 2008, girls were only one point behind. The older girls haven't changed in relation to the boys one way or the other. In 2004, 17-year-old boys averaged only three points ahead of the girls, but the girls in 2008 are just about where they were in 1982. You will note that the differences in reading scores are much greater.

The point is that there really isn't any reason why most girls can't do well in math other than they don't think that they will (Caplan & Caplan, 2005). Research shows clearly that many girls do poorly at math simply because they believe that math is hard for girls (Huguet & Régner, 2007; Spencer, Steele, & Quinn, 1999). If you believe that you cannot succeed at a task, you probably are not going to do well. You may also not succeed if you suffer from *stereotype threat*. This is the situation in which a person does poorly in a subject because other people who are similar to them do poorly. The idea is that if that person does well, their success threatens other members of their group. For example, boys may not work at learning to read if they believe that boys have trouble learning to read and that a boy who does read may be seen as not much of a boy. One suggestion for helping girls do better at math is to tell them about this influence and assure them that there is no reason that they cannot succeed at math (Inzlicht & Ben-Zeev, 2003; Johns, Schmader, & Martens, 2005).

Parents also contribute to girls' beliefs that they cannot do math (Frome & Eccles, 1998; Jacobs & Bleeker, 2004). When a girl has trouble in math, her friends and family may assure her that she should not worry because girls are not supposed to do well in math (Kurtz-Costes, Rowley, Harris-Britt, & Woods, 2008). This is an area where teachers can provide a lot of help by providing positive role models and by assuring girls that they can succeed (James, 2009).

Boys also have trouble in math, but there has not been much focus on this problem. Because boys believe that they are supposed to be able to do well in math, they can react badly when they have trouble in the subject. We have seen boys who have "lost" their textbook or homework, "forgotten" to take their assignment home or bring their completed homework back to class, or get upset or angry when faced with their math shortcomings. Math and science are part of the male academic domain, and boys tend to rate their abilities high in these areas (Sullivan, 2009). Consequently, when faced with failure or learning difficulties, boys will tend to blame the teacher for the problem instead of admitting that this is an area which is hard for them.

So why do children have trouble with math? There are several reasons, but three stand out.

1. *Dyscalculia:* This is also referred to as *math disability* and occurs equally in boys and girls (Shalev, 2004). Dyscalculia is seen in conjunction with other learning disabilities as well as by itself and is specifically a discrepancy between the individual's general cognitive ability and performance on mathematic tasks (Wadlington & Wadlington, 2008). It can be hard to diagnose because it may be overlooked in individuals who have other learning disabilities. For example, does a child have trouble with math because he cannot do the math, or is it that he cannot read the directions? Problems with one of three types of memory seem to be the cause of dyscalculia: The individual may not be able to recall numbers or math facts, to understand or recall math procedures, or to remember information presented spatially such as on graphs or tables (Geary, 2000).

2. *Poor background in math:* For a wide range of reasons, some students do not receive all of the instruction in basic math facts, procedures, and problem-solving techniques necessary to do well in class. Children change school districts as their families move, have illnesses which keep them from attending school, and may be suspended from attending classes for disciplinary purposes; these are just a few of the many reasons that children may not be present for instruction. Even if a child does receive instruction, not all students are able to learn from every teacher. Just because a child was present in class and did the work does not mean that the information will be available to her later.

3. *Math anxiety or phobia:* Some students will report that they are so anxious in math class that they are unable to learn the material. Most of these students will be girls, and the problem is the way in which they deal with stress (James, 2009). Most children will react to stress by *fight-or-flight,* in which blood floods the muscles and brain so that the individual is ready to run or to fight the oncoming threat. That may result in inappropriate behavior, but the child can think. Some children will react in an entirely different manner and their blood will go to the center of their body; they will be unable to move, unable to think, and they may cry or get nauseated. The solution is for the student to learn to identify the symptoms of this reaction, called *tend-and-befriend,* and to purposefully relax her body, which will result in the blood flooding back into the muscles and brain. This is easier said than done, but one crucial point is for the student to understand that the reaction is normal.

When a child does poorly in your math class, the first step is to try to find out what is the source of the problem—does the child have a learning disability in math or does the child lack vital information? In either case, presentation of the material using an active method will increase the chance that the student will be better able to remember and understand the concepts. For the anxious child, active approaches to learning will allow blood to flow back into the muscles and the child may relax or at least be better able to function in class. For the child who lacks information, active lessons allow the student to figure out what information is needed to solve the problem is missing.

True, math class has lots of opportunity for activities, and that is why many boys do well in math. Their high activity level and preference for kinesthetic (hands-on) and iconic (pictorial) learning fits well into the math classroom. However, if the teacher spends a great deal of time talking about the material, boys may lose focus and fail to learn the material. Increasing the number of activities will help boys stay focused in class. You will also find some girls who will thrive with a more active approach to math.

Most girls, on the other hand, generally prefer verbal (words) and auditory (hearing) learning activities, so it would seem that experiential learning would not suit them. Interestingly enough, when girls are given practical applications for math, they are able to relate the concepts to their own experience and it is easier for them to understand the process (James, 2009). They may, however, resist getting involved in active approaches to math, and you may need to convince them to try these lessons. One of the biggest issues that many girls have is that they are very concerned that they get the "right" answer and in experiential lessons, there may be several different approaches to solve the problem (James, 2009).

For all students, hands-on activities in math class give students the opportunity to apply problem solving techniques in novel ways. Learning math not only involves acquiring math facts, but also requires the student to apply those facts to different problems and in different ways. Good problem-solving and attack skills help students apply the facts they learn to a variety of problems, helping them learn to solve all sorts of problems. Classroom work alone does not always offer the chance for students to come up with their own approaches to a problem. A hands-on approach will make them better students.

Interactive math activities help students to

- focus in class,
- use additional avenues of learning,
- practice problem solving, and
- apply what they have learned to real-world (or what seem like real-world) situations.

Lesson 1

12-SIDED or 20-SIDED DIE TOSS

Topic: 12-Sided Die Toss is for younger students or for when there is no need for larger numbers. 20-Sided Die Toss is for older students or when more numbers are needed.

Purpose: To practice the basic computation of integers, fractions, and percents, ratios, squares and square roots, probability, and coordinate pairs; to select problems for homework and quiz incentives; and to release energy in exercise

Time: About 10 minutes

Materials:

- Pencil; paper; graph paper
- 12-sided die (available at www.enasco.com, item #TB21649T)
- 20-sided die (available at www.enasco.com, item #TB21243T)
- Giant Soft Foam Cubes—Operations (available at www.enasco.com, item #TB16935J). This item is optional for order of operations activities.

Procedure:

Skill practice

1. Demonstrate the mathematical skill or procedure used in the die toss, explaining how many points will be awarded for correct answers and the order in which the ball will be tossed.

2. Toss out the ball.

3. Student catches it with both hands and says the number or numbers under his thumbs.

4. Student performs one of the suggested tasks.

   Task 1: Add, subtract or multiply the numbers.

   Task 2: Make a fraction out of the numbers and reduce. Advanced groups will also change to decimals and percents. "4/5 is 0.8 or 80%."

   Task 3: Make a fraction and read it aloud, as in "the probability of 3 out of 5" or "odds are 2 out of 3."

   Task 4: Call out one number and square it: "10 squared is 100 and the square root of 100 is 10."

   Task 5: Call out the two numbers under his thumbs, one for x and one for y. Students plot coordinate pairs on graph paper or whiteboards. Use playing cards, dice, or foam cubes to determine positive and negative coordinates. Algebra students use numbers for slope and intercepts in the slope-intercept form.

   Task 6: Compute order of operations with several levels of difficulty. Teacher tosses. Student calls out number. Students record number on individual papers or whiteboards. Teacher or student rolls operation cube. Student tosses to another student and gives the answer or continues the toss and rolls. The level of difficulty is increased with tosses around the room mixing operations and numbers.

Homework or quiz incentives

1. Before you give out homework or a quiz, toss the ball.

2. After students call out number, say, "You don't have to do Problem 3 and Problem10, or if you do solve them they're each worth double if correct."

Energy release games

1. Students are in rows or lines ready to play game similar to Mother, May I.

2. Toss the ball.

3. Student catches the ball, reads number and asks, "Teacher, may we do 4 jumping jacks? May we take 6 baby steps back? May we run in place and count to 11?"

Evaluation: Do this activity to keep students' attention and promote quick response for mathematical processes. One die toss session typically lasts 10 minutes. It is excellent to use during the last 5 to 10 minutes of class. The 12-Sided or 20-Sided Die Toss is an interactive, movement-based activity that engages students in mathematical thinking. It uses rapid-fire recall of math facts, develops quick thinking of basic operations of the number system, and promotes studying of concepts in preparation for a high-stress activity that is competitive. The toss allows the teacher to give direct questions to an engaged group. Students feel smart because they can achieve a correct response quickly. If they answer incorrectly, they are actively listening to give a correct response the next time to regain loss from a previous error.

Lesson 2

FRACTION BARS

Purpose: Provide awareness of patterns in fractions or as a review for reducing fractions, fraction equivalencies, changing fractions to decimals and percents. Many students find it easier to remember fraction, decimals, and percents when they have a visual pattern to associate the fraction and equivalencies. Students can use the fraction bars for individual practice or partner practice.

Time: About 35 to 40 minutes

Materials: Fraction bars worksheet; scissors; straightedge or ruler for reducing and recognizing equivalent fractions. Optional: a book to hold fraction tree in place; cellophane tape.

Procedure:

Basic fraction practice

Students cut out each rectangle from the worksheet and fold horizontally along the dotted line to form a two-sided "bar." The long sides of the rectangle can be taped together, although this is not necessary.

Each bar will have a fraction or fractions on one side and the equivalent decimal and percentage values in the same positions on the other side. Students will use these like flash cards, flipping them over to practice individually or with a partner to develop rote skills with fraction-decimal equivalencies. For example, student asks partner: "What is the decimal for one half? What is the probability of 3 out of 4? 83% is what fraction?"

Reducing fractions and equivalent fractions: Build a fraction tree

Students form the base of the fraction tree by placing the one twelfth fraction bar at the near edge of their desktop or tabletop, fraction side up. They then align the one eighth bar just above the one twelfth bar, and continue with the same pattern, until the one half bar forms the top of the tree. (Optional: put the edge of each fraction bar under a book to hold in place or tape the tree into a notebook. Student is given extra copy of fraction bars for reference and flip practice.)

Students use a straightedge to check equivalent fractions down a vertical line. For example: 1/4, 2/8, and 3/12 are in a vertical line showing that they are equivalent fractions.

Students compare fractions with the vertical line. 3/8 is larger than 2/6 but smaller than 5/12. Students can then build a decimal tree and question each other as to what the fractions are which are hidden.

For older students, give them the fraction-decimal equivalencies for fractions with denominators of 7, 9, and 11; have them make their own Fraction Bars for all numbers 1 through 12. They should have no trouble making the one fifth bar.

When to Use: Fraction bars are used to introduce equivalencies of fractions or as a review activity.

Evaluation: The fraction bar is used as a structured activity that allows for kinesthetic learning and provides a visual representation of fraction equivalencies. The fraction tree and flip bars help students develop recall and problem-solving skills.

MATH LESSONS:
General Math

EXTRA INFORMATION ON TRANSFORMING FRACTIONS TO DECIMAL EQUIVALENTS

Students are familiar with the patterns of turning fractions with denominators of even numbers or five into their decimal equivalents, but it is more difficult to determine the decimal equivalents for 1/7, 1/9, and 1/11. Once students see these patterns, it will be easy for them to remember them.

Sevenths

The first step is for students to remember the following multiplication facts:

$2 \times 7 = 14$

$4 \times 7 = 28$

$8 \times 7 = 56$ (for the purposes of this pattern, 56 becomes 57 due to rounding up)

Show students the first three of these decimals and then see if they can determine the other three:

1/7 = .142857	4/7 = .571428
2/7 = .285714	5/7 = .714285
3/7 = .428571	6/7 = .857142

The pattern is not consistent, but with exposure, students will easily remember how to determine the decimal equivalent of sevenths.

Ninths

This is very easy; the decimal equivalent is simply the numerator times 11. For numbers five and higher, the last number can be rounded up.

1/9 = .111$\overline{1}$	5/9 = .555$\overline{5}$
2/9 = .222$\overline{2}$	6/9 = .666$\overline{6}$
3/9 = .333$\overline{3}$	7/9 = .777$\overline{7}$
4/9 = .444$\overline{4}$	8/9 = .888$\overline{8}$

Elevenths

This is also easy; the decimal equivalent is the numerator times 9 and also creates a repeating decimal, as does the pattern for ninths.

1/11 = .09$\overline{09}$	6/11 = .54$\overline{54}$
2/11 = .18$\overline{18}$	7/11 = .63$\overline{63}$
3/11 = .27$\overline{27}$	8/11 = .72$\overline{72}$
4/11 = .36$\overline{36}$	9/11 = .81$\overline{81}$
5/11 = .45$\overline{45}$	10/11 = .90$\overline{90}$

FR4–SQUARE STRATEGY Examples

$\frac{1}{6}$	$\frac{2}{6}$	$\frac{3}{6}$	$\frac{4}{6}$	$\frac{5}{6}$	$\frac{6}{6}$
.166	.333	.5	.666	.833	1
17%	33%	50%	67%	83%	100%

$\frac{1}{3}$	$\frac{2}{3}$	$\frac{3}{3}$
.333	.666	1
33%	67%	100%

$\frac{1}{12}$	$\frac{2}{12}$	$\frac{3}{12}$	$\frac{4}{12}$	$\frac{5}{12}$	$\frac{6}{12}$	$\frac{7}{12}$	$\frac{8}{12}$	$\frac{9}{12}$	$\frac{10}{12}$	$\frac{11}{12}$	$\frac{12}{12}$
.083	.166	.25	.333	.416	.50	.583	.666	.75	.833	.916	1
8.3%	**17%**	**25%**	**33%**	**42%**	**50%**	**58%**	**67%**	**75%**	**83%**	**92%**	**100%**

$\frac{1}{2}$	$\frac{2}{2}$
.5	1
50%	100%

$\frac{1}{4}$	$\frac{2}{4}$	$\frac{3}{4}$	$\frac{4}{4}$
.25	.50	.75	1
25%	50%	75%	100%

$\frac{1}{8}$	$\frac{2}{8}$	$\frac{3}{8}$	$\frac{4}{8}$	$\frac{5}{8}$	$\frac{6}{8}$	$\frac{7}{8}$	$\frac{8}{8}$
.125	.25	.375	.5	.625	.75	.875	1
12.5%	25%	37.5%	50%	62.5%	75%	87.5%	100%

$\frac{1}{10}$	$\frac{2}{10}$	$\frac{3}{10}$	$\frac{4}{10}$	$\frac{5}{10}$	$\frac{6}{10}$	$\frac{7}{10}$	$\frac{8}{10}$	$\frac{9}{10}$	$\frac{10}{10}$
.10	.20	.30	.40	.50	.60	.70	.80	.90	1
10%	20%	30%	40%	50%	60%	70%	80%	90%	100%

Lesson 3

CASTING OUT NINES

Level: Student level varies with level of math (review: proofreading math)

Purpose: To learn a method for proofreading arithmetic calculations. (Active learners have a hard time proofreading because they have a hard time focusing on details. Any method that is more active than just scanning work already done will help students be more efficient in finding errors. This is an old method to check work, but it works, and it gives students an active method to confirm their answers.)

Time: To teach this takes several minutes, but the point is for students to use this method to check their work. It won't add much to the time students take to finish a problem.

Materials: Accompanying worksheet to learn the skill. Once learned, the strategy can be used on any work to be handed in.

Procedure:

Addition

Casting out nines can be used to check a long addition problem. Add together all the digits in each horizontal row of the calculation. Then add the sums from each addend (each row above the line) together. Do the same for the bottom row (the final sum). Continue adding the digits in double-digit numbers together until you have a single-digit number. You "cast out" or cross out all nines and numbers that add up to nine. Then add the numbers above the line together. They should equal the number obtained from the sum.

Example:

$$361 \rightarrow 3 + 6 = \cancel{9} \text{ Cast out, left with } 1$$
$$245 \rightarrow 4 + 5 = \cancel{9} \text{ Cast out, left with } 2 \Bigg\} = 1 + 8 = \cancel{9} \text{ Cast out, left with } 2$$
$$+\ 719 \rightarrow \text{ Cast out } \cancel{9}, 7 + 1 = \qquad\qquad 8$$
$$\overline{}$$
$$1325 \rightarrow 3 + 1 + 2 + 5 = 11, 1 + 1 = 2 \qquad\qquad 2 = 2$$

Subtraction

This works the same way that addition works but at the end you subtract the subtrahend from the minuend, and that will equal the numbers for the difference. If the number for the minuend is smaller than that for the subtrahend, add 9 for the minuend.

$$2460 \rightarrow 2 + 4 + 6 = 12,\ 1 + 2 = 3 \Big\} \text{ Since you can't subtract 8 from 3,}$$
$$-\ 539 \rightarrow \text{ Cast out } \cancel{9}, 5 + 3 \qquad = 8 \Big\} \text{ add 9 to the 3 so } 12 - 8 = 4$$
$$\overline{}$$
$$1921 \rightarrow \text{ Cast out } \cancel{9}, 1 + 2 + 1 = 4 \qquad\qquad 4 = 4$$

Multiplication

Again, the check works the same way except that you multiply the numbers obtained from the two multipliers to compare to the number obtained from the answer.

$$256 \rightarrow 2 + 5 + 6 = 13,\ 1 + 3 = 4$$
$$\times\ 26 \rightarrow 2 + 6 \qquad\qquad\quad = 8\ \Big\}\ 4 \times 8 = 32,\ 3 + 2 = 5$$

$$6656 \rightarrow 6 + 6 + 6 = 18,\ 1 + 8 = \cancel{9},\ \text{cast out left with 5} \qquad\qquad 5 = 5$$

Division

This check works for long division as well. Find single digit numbers for divisor, dividend, quotient, and remainder, if any. Multiply the divisor by the quotient and add in the remainder. That number should equal the number for the dividend.

$$\begin{array}{r} 14 \\ 26\overline{)381} \end{array}\ \text{r}17$$

Divisor is $2 + 6 = 8$,

Quotient is $1 + 4 = 5$,

Multiply divisor and quotient $5 \times 8 = 40$

Add in remainder $40 + 17 = 57 = 5 + 7 = 12 = 1 + 2 = 3$

Dividend is $8 + 1 = 9$, cast out, left with 3

$$3 = 3$$

Evaluation: After several times through using this method, students should be able to reliably check their answers to math problems.

CASTING OUT 9s Worksheet

Name: _____

Addition problems

```
    2 3              2 7 9
    8 0                5 3
  + 6 7              1 0 0 6
  -------          +   8 3 1
    1 7 0          ---------
                     2 1 6 0
```

Subtraction problems

```
    4 3 6            9 2 0 3
  -   7 3          -     2 6
  -------          ---------
    3 6 3            9 1 7 7
```

Multiplication problem

```
      7 4
    × 3 5
    ------
    3 7 0
    2 2 2
    ------
    2 5 9 0
```

Division problem

```
          7 5
    2 3)1 7 4 2  r 1 7
```

CASTING OUT 9s Worksheet (Answers)

MATH LESSONS:
General Math

Addition problems

$$\left.\begin{array}{r} 23 = 5 \\ 80 = 8 \\ + \ 67 = 13, 1 + 3 = 4 \end{array}\right\} 5 + 8 + 4 = 17, 1 + 7 = \mathbf{8}$$

$$\overline{170} = 1 + 7 = \mathbf{8}$$

$$\left.\begin{array}{rll} 27\cancel{9} = 7 + 2 & = \cancel{9} \\ 53 = 5 + 3 & = 8 \\ 1006 = 1 + 6 & = 7 \\ + \ 831 = 8 + 1 & = \cancel{9}, 3 \end{array}\right\} \begin{array}{l} 8 + 7 + 3 = 18 \\ \rightarrow 8 + 1 = \cancel{9} = 0 \end{array}$$

$$\overline{2160} = 2 + 1 + 6 = 9 = \mathbf{0}$$

Subtraction problems

$$\left.\begin{array}{rl} 436 = 3 + 6 & = \cancel{9}, 4 \\ - \ 73 = 7 + 3 = 10, 1 + 0 = 1 \end{array}\right\} \begin{array}{l} 4 + 1 + \mathbf{3} \end{array}$$

$$\overline{363} = 3 + 6 + 3 = 12, 1 + 2 + \mathbf{3}$$

$$\left.\begin{array}{rl} \cancel{9}203 = 2 + 3 & = 5 \\ - \ 26 = 2 + 6 & = 8 \end{array}\right\} \begin{array}{l} 5 - 8 \ (\text{borrow } 9) \\ \rightarrow 14 - 8 = 6 \end{array}$$

$$\overline{\cancel{9}177} = 1 + 7 + 7 = 15, 1 + 5 = \mathbf{6}$$

Multiplication problem

$$\left.\begin{array}{r} 74 = 7 + 4 = 11, 1 + 1 = 2 \\ \times 35 = 3 + 5 = \ 8 \end{array}\right\} \begin{array}{l} 2 \times 8 = 16 \\ \rightarrow 1 + 6 = \ \mathbf{7} \end{array}$$

$$\overline{370}$$
$$222$$
$$\overline{2590} = 2 + 5 = \mathbf{7}$$

Division problem

$$23\overline{)1742}^{\ 75} \text{ r17}$$

Divisor: $2 + 3 = 5$

Quotient: $7 + 5 = 12 \rightarrow 1 + 2 = 3$

Multiply: $5 \times 3 = 15 \rightarrow 1 + 5 = 6$

Remainder: $1 + 7 = 8$

Add: $6 + 8 = 14 \rightarrow 1 + 4 = \mathbf{5}$

Dividend: $1 + 7 + 4 + 2 = 14 \rightarrow 1 + 4 = \mathbf{5}$

Lesson 4
I'M NOT IRRATIONAL!

Level: For both older and younger students—two worksheets provided (lesson: connect math and verbal skills)

Purpose: To reduce confusion about mathematical terms by analyzing how the words have a mathematical and everyday English usage

Time: Three days to interview. One class period to record, discuss, and analyze how the words have both a mathematical and an everyday English usage.

Materials:

- Seven copies of survey for each student, in case they let slip what the survey is really about
- Charts around the room for students to record or tally responses

Procedure:

1. Each student should receive seven copies of the worksheet

2. Directions for students

    A. Interview five people who are not students in school (any school, not just yours—college is OK). You may interview teachers, but they should not be science or math teachers.

    B. Record their comment or sentence on the chart. If the participant's answers are related to math, that is OK. Do not tell them it's a math project. If you slip up and say that it is a math project, just document it, but you must find another person to replace the one who was told.

    C. The last column will be completed in class.

3. When students come to class, display the words in some way in the classroom, either by writing them on a board or on a large piece of paper.

4. Students will then write the meanings that they have collected beneath the words, keeping track of similar answers.

5. The class will decide whether the answers fit a math definition or some other definition and will mark their answer sheets accordingly.

6. Students will discuss how the math and non-math definitions of the words differ or are similar.

7. Challenge students to come up with other words that have two meanings, one in math and one in another context.

Evaluation: This exercise is designed to help students understand how the meanings of words used in mathematics can be confused when the words are used in other ways. You could include items on the next test to evaluate their understanding of these words, but that is not the intention of this exercise.

MATH LESSONS:
General Math

I'M NOT IRRATIONAL! Worksheet (older students)

Name: _____

Read these directions:

I am doing a survey for school on the meaning of 10 words. I will say a word. Please give me a definition or a sentence using the word. I will record your answer. Thank you for participating.

Word	Participant's comment or sentence	Fit?
Origin		
Reflection		
Product		
Median		
Power		
Function		
Acute		
Prime		
Variable		
Irrational		

I'M NOT IRRATIONAL! Worksheet (younger students)

Name: _____

Read these directions:

I am doing a survey for school on the meaning of five words. I will say a word. Please give me a definition or a sentence using the word. I will record your answer. Thank you for participating.

Word	Participant's comment or sentence	Fit?
Times		
Borrow		
Divide		
Average		
Difference		

Lesson 5

PEMDAS (Parentheses, Exponents, Multiplication, Division, Addition, Subtraction)

Level: For students needing work on order of operations (review)

Purpose: To ensure that all students have a solid understanding of the order of operations. Additionally, students will develop problem-solving skills that will help them develop equations from word problems. Sometimes older students have trouble with this concept, so if you suspect that this may be an issue, try giving out worksheets to take home. A lack of solid understanding of the order of operations is at the bottom of many problems that students have when they move to scientific calculators.

Time: About 10 minutes, when used as an end-of-the-day competitive game. Can also be used as homework for more complicated problems, which may take longer.

Materials: Math problems from your textbook or other sources. Prepare the problems by typing or writing the numbers involved in the equation in order, but removing all notation.

Procedure:

1. Begin by putting a problem on the board and showing students what the problem is asking them to do. Then give the class simple equations to solve.

2. Prepare worksheets ahead of time, or display problems on the board for students to solve.

3. If this is a competition, do not allow students to blurt out the answers. There are several different methods you can use to run a competition.

    a. Each student can have an individual whiteboard. He will write his solution on the board, then hold it up so that only you can see it. If the answer is correct, he moves on to the next problem.

    b. If students need a more active version of this game, provide slips of paper with the problems on them. The students work either in pairs or individually. Pass out the strips face down. When each student has one, tell them to turn the papers over and "get solving." When a student or pair of students has an answer, they are to bring the solution to the teacher. If the answer is correct, they get another problem to solve. If the answer is not correct, the student or students return to their desk to see if they can find a solution. If after two tries, they cannot, they move on to a new problem and get no points for the missed problem.

    c. If you have the students bring their answers to you, they must line up in order, or you will have differences of opinion as to who was first.

    d. Award points based on completion of problems in the first or second attempt.

    e. If there is more than one solution, you can award points to the students who find all of the solutions, or tell the students that there is more than one solution and challenge them to find all of the solutions.

Evaluation: As students get better at this game, they will make fewer order-of-operation mistakes in problems.

PEMDAS Sample Worksheet

Name: _____

Simple problems:

1. 3 __ 7 __ 10

2. 5 __ 3 __ 2

3. 10 __ 4 __ 6

4. 3 __ 4 __ 8 __ 1 __ 35

More complex problems:

5. 5 __ 7 __ __ 2

6. 4 __ 3 __ 1 __ __ 8

7. 2 __ 6 __ 3 __ __ 4

8. __ 12 __ __ 3 _ 4 __ __ __ 13

Algebra-level problems:

9. 0 __ 10 __ 0

10. 2 __ 2y __ 6y __ __ 16y

11. 3x __ 4y __ __ __ 6x __ __ 4y __ 9x

12. __ y __ 1 __ __ y __ 2 __ __ y^2 __ 3y __ 2

MATH LESSONS:
General Math

PEMDAS Sample Worksheet (Answers)

Simple problems:

Problems	Answers
1. 3 __ 7 __ 10	$3 + 7 = 10$
2. 5 __ 3 __ 2	$5 - 3 = 2$ or $5 = 3 + 2$
3. 10 __ 4 __ 6	$10 = 4 + 6$ or $10 - 4 = 6$
4. 3 __ 4 __ 8 __ 1 __ 36	$3 + 48 + 1 = 36$

More complex problems:

Problems	Answers
5. 5 __ 7 __ __ 2	$5 - 7 = -2$ or $5 = 7 + -2$
6. 4 __ 3 __ 1 __ __ 8	$4(3 - 1) = 8$
7. 2 __ 6 __ 3 __ __ 4	$2(6 \div 3) = 4$
8. __ 12 __ __ 3 __ 4 __ __ __ 13	$-12 + (3 - 4) = -13$

Algebra level problems:

Problems	Answers
9. 0 __ 10 __ 0	$0 \times 10 = 0$ or $0 \div 10 = 0$ (reversing the signs is a major error)
10. 2__ __ 2y __ 6y __ __ 16y	$2(2y + 6y) = 16y$
11. 3x __ 4y __ __ __ 6x __ __ 4y __ 9x	$3x - 4y - (-6x) + 4y = 9x$
12. __ y __ 1 __ __ y __ 2 __ __ y2 __ 3y __ 2	$(y + 1)(y + 2) = y2 + 3y + 2$

Lesson 6
SCHOOL STATISTICS

Level: Can be adapted for many levels (lesson)

Purpose: To introduce the concept of spread sheets, data collection, and graphical representation of data

Time: About 30 minutes per session over several weeks

Materials:

- Computer with spreadsheet software
- Rulers; meter sticks; measuring tapes; scales (large and small)
- Graph paper

Procedure:

1. Help the students explore what sort of data is easily available from the school. This can include information on the building itself, the contents of the building, the grounds around the building, the staff and faculty, the students, or anything else that can be measured, counted, or weighed.

2. Have students decide what data they will collect. Guide students to collect items of data that are related, such as the number of chairs in a room and the number of students in a room. Students will decide how extensive the data collection will be. Will data be collected only from their own class, from their own hall, or from the entire school? For more advanced students, a comparison of data from one class with data for the whole school will illustrate the difference between sample and population.

3. Students will then develop a data collection sheet. Teacher should assign students to different collection groups. A time frame for completion of this task should be established, as some of the collection may take place outside of class time.

4. Elementary level students can display information using squares of colored paper glued to a large graph to make bar graphs. Each square can represent one individual who is being counted. For example, a graph of the heights of the members of the class would have a number line with the appropriate heights along the bottom, and the students can paste a square for each student above the corresponding height.

5. Using the spreadsheet software, students will develop a matrix for the data being collected. As the students complete their data collection process, they will enter the data into the spreadsheet.

6. The spreadsheet software is activated and data obtained.

7. Students should produce graphs of the data and write an analysis of the results.

8. Advanced students should be shown how to do this on a TI-83 calculator.

Evaluation: This lesson requires active involvement in the collection of data and gives students a visual frame of reference for the results. Experiential learners are better able to focus on activities when the lesson requires that the student engage in the lesson. Also, for students who are better at visualizing information, the graphs produced by the data analysis software give pictorial representations of the data.

Lesson 7
STOCK MARKET GAME

Level: For students familiar with matrices (enrichment: math, economics, civics)

Purpose: To use information from the stock market to demonstrate how to display information in matrices and to use matrices to calculate changes in data

Time: 20 minutes twice a week

Materials: Worksheets and/or spreadsheet software for more advanced students

Procedure:

1. Select three stocks and note what the stock sold for that day.

2. Students are to record their stocks for 8 or 10 days in the matrices using the following worksheet. Each day they should write a sentence telling whether the stock's price moved up or down and by how much. They may write it below the chart or on another piece of paper. On the last day, they add their totals and tell how much they gained or lost during the project period. Then they are to write a summary of the project. Include the following information: the names of the stocks and why they were chosen, where they got their information, what they learned, and at least one sentence from a family member about their work.

3. Students should use the point value worksheet to calculate their score on this project.

4. In several months, you may want to revisit this project. Students should select the same stocks as in the original project and calculate change.

5. The matrices sheet is for upper level students who are studying that concept. For all other students, the stock market project sheet is sufficient. Students who are using matrices will select one of their stocks to analyze in this fashion.

Evaluation: Money always makes math more fun. Learning to determine whether stock prices go up or down, and by how much, is interesting to active learners. Competing to be the class stockbroker will also make this exercise more enjoyable. Additionally, students have practice dealing with matrices and spread sheets.

POINT VALUE FOR INVESTMENT PROJECT, 10 DAYS

Directions for students:

Day 1–10 matrices: Must include previous day, new day, and difference of the two matrices showing gains or losses.

Scalar matrices: Must include gains or losses multiplied by 100 shares. Total gain or loss for all four stocks is shown on paper with a sentence that states profit or loss for the day. Example: "On Day 1, I was up $124.00." or "On Day 2, I was down by $42.00."

(50 points, 5 per day)

Written report to include three paragraphs. (total: 50 points)

Section 1

- Why you chose each one of your stocks. (12 points)
- The official name of the stock, not just abbreviation. (4 points)

Section 2

- What you learned about matrices and daily change in stock values (you may add parent comments). (12 points)

Section 3

- An explanation of how to make a matrix to record values of stocks; describe the process that you did every day to determine profit and loss in your stocks. (12 points)
- Organized portfolio folder to include project description paper, matrices, and written portion with signatures. (10 points)

Due dates for each paragraph section

In class: Section 1—Why you chose each stock and the correct name in a paragraph.

Two days later: Section 2—What you learned about matrices and daily change in stock values with family comments in a paragraph.

One week later: Section 3—Turn in completed project in the portfolio with a paragraph describing the process of recording stocks in a matrix.

STOCK MARKET PROJECT, 8 DAYS

Name:_____ Date started: _____ Date due: _____

Directions: Check your stocks for a 1-month period. Check the prices twice a week and record the data in the chart. You may use the newspaper or the website www.sectorspdr.com. Subtract the difference between the day's close and record the difference as a gain (+) or a loss (−). Multiply by 100. Add your gains and losses. Record the totals A through G in the last column.

Each day write a sentence stating if you were up or down for the day. The first one is started for you below. Then write a summary about your stocks and what you learned.

STOCKS:

Name				
Symbol				

Sample: On day 2 my total was up by $23.00. On day 2 my total was down by −$13.00.

Total A Day 2 _____

Total B Day 3_____

Total C Day 4_____

Total D Day 5_____

Total E Day 6_____

Total F Day 7_____

Total G Day 8_____

My overall total for the month was $_____

Write a description on lined paper about the stock project. Include the names of your stocks and why you chose them, where you got your information, what you learned, and at least one sentence from a family member about your work. Staple all papers, fold and turn in with date completed.

Good luck in the market!

We will check our stocks on the same day of each month until the end of school.

Day 1					
Day 2					
Gain or loss					
× 100 shares					Total A
Day 2					
Day 3					
Gain or loss					
× 100 shares					Total B
Day 3					
Day 4					
Gain or loss					
× 100 shares					Total C
Day 4					
Day 5					
Gain or loss					
× 100 shares					Total D
Day 5					
Day 6					
Gain or loss					
× 100 shares					Total E
Day 6					
Day 7					
Gain or loss					
× 100 shares					Total F
Day 7					
Day 8					
Gain or loss					
× 100 shares					Total G
Daily total	AB	BC	CD	Total row	
	DE	EF	FG	Total row	

STOCK MARKET PROJECT, 10 DAYS

Name: _____

Record one of your stocks for 10 days in the matrices below. Each day write a sentence telling if the total value of your stock was up or down and by how much. You may write it below the chart or on another piece of paper. On the last day add your totals and tell how much you gained or lost during the project period. Then write a summary of the project. Include the following information: the names of your stock and why you chose this one to examine, where you got your information, what you learned, and at least one sentence from a family member about your work.

Good luck in the market!

Day 1 [   ]

Day 2 [   ] - [   ] = [   ] 100 [   ]

Day 3 [   ] - [   ] = [   ] 100 [   ]

Day 4 [   ] - [   ] = [   ] 100 [   ]

Day 5 [   ] - [   ] = [   ] 100 [   ]

Day 6 [   ] - [   ] = [   ] 100 [   ]

Day 7 [   ] - [   ] = [   ] 100 [   ]

Day 8 [   ] - [   ] = [   ] 100 [   ]

Day 9 [   ] - [   ] = [   ] 100 [   ]

Day 10 [   ] - [   ] = [   ] 100 [   ]

Lesson 8

WHETHER WEATHER

Level: Can be adapted for many levels (enrichment: math, science, geography)

Purpose: To introduce the concept of spread sheets, data collection, and graphical representation of data

Time: About 30 minutes per session over several weeks

Materials:
- Computer with spreadsheet software
- Graph paper
- Data collection forms and/or access to Internet
- Map of the United States

Procedure:

Basic students

1. Students will use data collection forms to gather data on local weather conditions. This exercise can be done in collaboration with a science unit on weather; a math/science joint project will make a bigger impact on students. If you like, you can have students select other areas of the world to collect weather data for the given period of time. Students will need to decide if they are going to collect data for 10 consecutive days, which will mean they need to collect data at home over the weekend, or if they want to collect data for two weeks at school only. You may want for some students to do one process and others to do the other and compare results.

2. Students will find the mean, median, and mode of all classes of data. Where appropriate, students will investigate the variability of results and calculate the standard deviation for those results.

3. Students will graph the data by hand and then use the spreadsheet software to do the same thing. The reason for doing the exercise first by hand is to give students a feeling for how data will look when graphed. *For experiential learners, this step is essential.* If you let the students only analyze the data by computer alone, they will punch the buttons and never pay attention to whether the results make sense or not.

4. Students will post their graphs and compare their results.

5. Where appropriate, students should be shown how to do this on a TI-83 calculator.

Advanced students

1. Students will use data from the Internet to locate all the tornadoes that were detected in the United States in a given year. You may want to give each group of students a different year so that they can compare their data at the end.

2. Students should overlay the map of the United States with a grid and mark on the grid the location of each tornado and the severity of the tornado as rated by the Fujita Tornado Damage Scale. This information is easily found on the Internet.

3. Students will then calculate the probability of a tornado appearing in any particular area of the United States. Students should also calculate the probability of the severity of a tornado in the most active areas.

4. Students will determine which areas of the United States are least likely and most likely to suffer tornado damage and which months are most active in each area.

5. Students can then use spreadsheets and statistical analysis software to analyze the data, producing graphical representations of the results.

Evaluation: This lesson requires active involvement in the collection of data and gives students a visual frame of reference for the results. Active learners are better able to focus on activities when the lesson requires that the student engage in the lesson. Also, for students who are better at visualizing information, the graphs produced by the data analysis software give pictorial representations of the data.

WEATHER DATA COLLECTION CHART

Name: _____

	Hi Temp C/F	Low Temp C/F	Precipitation	Humidity	Barometric Pressure	Wind Direction	Average Wind Speed
Day 1							
Day 2							
Day 3							
Day 4							
Day 5							
Day 6							
Day 7							
Day 8							
Day 9							
Day 10							

WEATHER MATRICES

Another exercise for basic students is to compare the temperature variations of various cities using a matrix.

Each student selects three cities in various parts of your state, your region, or the United States. Students then use the Internet to find out the high and low temperatures for each city for previous day and put that data in the first matrix. They then find the average high and low temperatures for the same day and put that data in the second matrix. All of this data will be easily found at www.wunderground.com for the cities selected by the students. The difference between the first two matrices will be put in the third matrix.

Actual	High	Low
City 1	[	]
City 2	[	]
City 3	[	]

Average	High	Low
City 1	[	]
City 2	[	]
City 3	[	]

Difference	High	Low
City 1	[	]
City 2	[	]
City 3	[	]

Lesson 9

FOUR-SQUARE STRATEGY

Level: Can be adapted for many levels, but start with pre-algebra (review: math)

Purpose: To organize and practice skills using verbal, graphic, and numerical reasoning

Time: About 10 to 30 minutes

Materials: Examples of the skill to be practiced; pencils; copies of Four-Square Strategy worksheets

Procedure:

1. Students fill in the four squares by following directions in the square.

2. Students may work with partners.

3. Students share with the class their solutions.

4. Students may highlight or take notes.

5. Students place the completed worksheets in notebook for reference.

Evaluation: Four-Square Strategy is used when introducing or reviewing a skill. Students have a chance to discuss procedures during seat work. It helps students see the different ways the same problem can be presented. It is helpful before a quiz as an organizer and is easy for teachers to produce for different skills.

Name: _____

Date _____

4-Square Strategy With Functions

Write the equation.	Make a table.
Graph the equation.	Write or draw a verbal description of the model.

Name: _____

Date _____

4-Square Strategy With Fractions

Write the fraction and draw a picture of your fraction.	Write a word problem with your fraction.
Change it to decimal.	Change it to a percent.

Lesson 10

BOX THE OPERATOR

Level: For pre-algebra and algebra (problem-solving skills: math)

Purpose: To help students solve word problems. Many children have trouble with word problems. Some have trouble *disembedding*, or finding the math among the words, while others have trouble translating words into the figures of a math equation. Box the Operator is a technique which will help all students succeed with word or story problems.

Time: 10 to 15 minutes (For students who already are familiar with word problems. If you introduce this along with word or story problems, the students will never know that there is any other way to look at these types of problems.)

Materials: Word problems from your textbook and from other sources

Procedure:

1. Identify the *operators*—all the words that indicate a mathematical operation. This will be easier if students keep a math dictionary in the back of their notebooks. Identifying the operators will help students see the difference between terms such as *divide by* and *divide into* and the similarity between terms such as *times* and *multiply*. As students identify the operators, they should highlight these words with a bright color such as neon yellow or green. The reason this technique is called Box the Operator is that before the invention of highlighters, students drew a box around the operators.

2. Identify all the *numbers,* whether they appear as digits or as words, and draw a red line under each number. As students get into more complicated problems, they should be careful to make sure that the numbers are part of the problem and not simply a red herring. Also, they should be careful to find numbers even if they do not seem like numbers. For example, if a problem states that Suzie and her brother go to buy apples, it may be important that two people are involved and it may not be. The student needs to determine if that is part of the problem.

3. Locate the *equality* in the problem. An equation means that there are two parts which are to be set as equals to each other and somewhere in the story is a phrase such as *is the same as, the final amount is, what is, how many,* and the like. Students can highlight the equality with a different color or can draw green arrows across it.

4. The next step is to find the *variables* and draw a circle around them with a pencil. As problems become more complicated, there may be several variables in the problem; all of the same kind of variables should be circled with the same color.

5. The last step is to write down just the parts of the problem that are marked. The equation will be very visible and easy for students to solve.

Evaluation: When students can accurately identify the major parts of a word problem, they have successfully completed this task.

BOX THE OPERATOR Example

Start with a simple problem such as this one:

If three times a number is increased by seven, the result is the same as when 72 is decreased by twice the number.

Step 1. Box the operator. Either highlight or draw a box around the words which indicate mathematical operations. You will note that half of *twice* is highlighted as it is both a number and an operation.

If three times a number is increased by seven, the result is the same as when 72 is decreased by twice the number.

Step 2. Identify all the numbers by underlining each in red. You will note that half of *twice* is underlined indicating the number part of the word.

If three times a number is increased by seven, the result is the same as when 72 is decreased by twice the number.

Step 3. Locate the equality in the problem. Either highlight with a different color or draw a large equals sign over the appropriate words.

If three times a number is increased by seven, the result is the same as when 72 is decreased by twice the number.

Step 4. Find the variables and draw a circle around them. Make sure that the variables refer to the same term.

If three times a number is increased by seven, the result is the same as when 72 is decreased by twice the number.

Step 5. Write the problem down as it is marked

$$3 \times N + 7 = 72 - 2 \times N$$

More traditional word problems may not need all of these steps, but marking the parts of the problem will help students.

This year, Bob saved $250 for his college fund. That amount represents 10% of what he made bagging groceries after school. How much did he make working at the grocery store?

$$\$250 = .10 \times W$$

It took Sam <u>1 1/2 hours</u> to mow his grandmother's lawn and it took him <u>half</u> as long to weed the flower bed in front of the house. If his grandmother pays him <u>$5.00</u> per hour, how much does he make each time he tidies up her yard?

In this sentence, *half* means to divide by two, so it refers to both a number and an operation. The amount of time spent weeding is the amount of time spent mowing divided by two. The first part then looks like: 1 1/2 + 1/2 (1 1/2)

The second part of problem is $5.00 × total hours spent = money earned: (1 1/2 + 1/2 (1 1/2)) × $5.00 = money earned

You will note that this problem requires either two steps—finding the total amount of time spent on yard work before multiplying by the hourly rate, or learning to set that part of the problem off with parentheses.

**MATH LESSONS:
Algebra**

Lesson 11

JUST A FIB

Level: Can be adapted for students pre-algebra and above (enrichment: math and language arts)

Purpose: To write a poem using the Fibonacci sequence

Time: About 10 to 30 minutes

Materials: Pencil; paper; Fibonacci sequence on the board; Just a Fib worksheet

Procedure:

1. Students are shown the pattern of the Fibonacci sequence and a sample poem.

2. Students compose a poem in which the number of words in each line is the number in that row of the sequence. To make it tougher, use the number of syllables, as in a haiku. Teacher gives the students permission to tell a big fib or be truthful.

   Do not start a sentence in the middle of a row.

3. Students share their Fibs with the class.

4. Students may design a border to fit inside the lines on the worksheet. It should have a pattern that is repeated around the border in colors or black and white. Students could use fractals or tessellations.

5. Place the Fibs on a bulletin board with brief history and picture of Fibonacci. (*Hint:* Ask your language arts teacher to check grammar rules if a creative student gets up to 21.)

   Sources of help: http://pass.maths.org.uk/issue3/fibonacci/index.html; http://www.newton.ac.uk/wmy2kposters/january

Examples:

Just a Fib

0

1 I

1 ran

2 home quickly

3 to see Tom.

5 He got a new bike

8 that has special tires for mountain climbing trips.

13 So my parents took us camping at Mount Mitchell State Park in July.

21 We had fun scaring all the birds and rabbits off the trails by throwing out rocks and dust with our tires.

Just a Fib

0

1 I

1 am

2 standing in

3 my math class

5 trying to write a Fib.

Evaluation: Fibs is a fun way to introduce patterns and number sequences. It is a nice activity for the first week of school. The display on the bulletin board is a simple example of creative writing across the curriculum. Enrichment websites show the squares and spirals with the Fibonacci sequence.

JUST A FIB

0

1

1

2

3

5

8

13

21

Signature

Date

Lesson 12
PEANUT STATISTICS

Level: Several levels (enrichment: math, statistics, science)

Purpose: To visually demonstrate the basics of statistics. The advantage of this lesson is that you can include as much or as little of the material as your students are ready for.

Time: About 60 minutes

Materials: Worksheet; small metric ruler; calculator; peanuts or copies of peanuts

Procedure:

1. Originally, this exercise used actual peanuts in the shell, but because of allergies, that is no longer possible. Find a place that sells peanuts in an open bin and scoop a large bag full. Each pair of students needs 20 peanuts, so multiply 20 by half the size of your largest class and that is how many peanuts in the shell you need. Make sure that you have a variety of peanuts, including very small ones and very large ones.

2. Line up 20 peanuts in the shell on a copying machine and make a copy of those peanuts. Do the same with the rest of your peanuts so that every pair of students has a sheet with a different batch of peanuts.

3. Hand out to each pair of students a worksheet, a peanut sheet, a ruler, and a calculator or have them provide their own calculators.

4. Students should measure the peanuts, end to end, putting the data on the sheet.

5. Students should graph the data for their sample of peanuts.

6. The data from all students should be collected either by the teacher or by a designated student. Using a calculator with a statistics function, determine the population data. The graph for the population can be drawn on the board or determined by the calculator.

7. Advanced students will calculate the deviation by subtracting the length of each peanut from the mean of the peanuts and then square the deviations. The sum of the deviations squared is the top term in the formula on the advanced sheet.

8. Discuss the relationship between each sample of peanuts and the population of peanuts. The discussion can vary depending on the math understanding of the students.

Evaluation: At the completion of this exercise, students should have an understanding of population, sample, random assignment, random selection, mean, median, and mode. More advanced students should have an understanding of variance and standard deviation.

PEANUT STATISTICS Worksheet (basic student)

Name: _____

Distribution of the length of 20 peanuts

Peanut (#)	Length (Centimeters [cm])
1	
2	
3	
4	
5	
6	
7	
8	
10	
11	
12	
13	
14	
15	
16	
17	
18	
19	
20	
Sum of lengths	
Mean	
Median	
Mode	

PEANUT STATISTICS Worksheet (advanced student)

Name: _____

Distribution of the length of 20 (N) peanuts

Peanut (#)	Length (Centimeters [cm])	Deviation	Deviation^2
1			
2			
3			
4			
5			
6			
7			
8			
10			
11			
12			
13			
14			
15			
16			
17			
18			
19			
20			
Sum of lengths			
Mean			
Median			
Mode			

MATH LESSONS:
Algebra

Standard deviation:

$$\sigma = \sqrt{\frac{\left(\sum(x - \bar{x})\right)^2}{n}}$$

$\sum$ = Greek letter *sigma* stands for sum. σ is the lower-case *sigma* and stands for standard deviation

$\sqrt{}$ = square root

n = number, the total number of items in the sample. For some cases, the number is n-1 or one less than the total number of items.

x = each item in the sample

$\bar{x}$ pronounced "x bar," stands for the mean of the population

The part of the formula which is contained in the parentheses $(x - \bar{x})$ is the same as the deviation.

Lesson 13

PROBLEM SOLVING WITH HOLMES

Level: Can be adapted for various levels, middle school and above (problem-solving skills: math, science)

Purpose: To provide an organized format for solving of word problems with multiple steps involving formulas and unit analysis. (It is best used with students in pairs.)

Time: About 30 minutes

Materials: One copy of Holmes worksheet per pair or per student; pencils; references for formulas and unit analysis; word problems

Procedure:

1. Give students copy of the Problem Solving With Holmes worksheet. Go over each section and ask students to explain how the section of the template could help them in problem solving.

2. Give students copy of word problem.

3. For advanced level, allow students to solve the word problem, filling in appropriate sections.

4. For average level students, break down the problem using the Box the Operator technique, then allow them to solve the word problem in pairs. Identifying formulas and conversions needed for the word problem may be necessary the first time the template is used.

5. Walk around the classroom, checking student work for accuracy.

6. Students share and justify answers using different sections and strategies of problem solving.

Evaluation: This is best used with multistep word problems containing diagrams, formulas, and conversions. Average and proficient learners like the organization of the format. It helps them to see what needs to done in order to find a solution. Advanced learners like the way the format quickly organizes more difficult information for problem solving. They can "see" where they are going.

Active students enjoy the idea of solving a challenging word problem by taking the role of Sherlock Holmes.

PROBLEM SOLVING WITH HOLMES

Name and date: _____

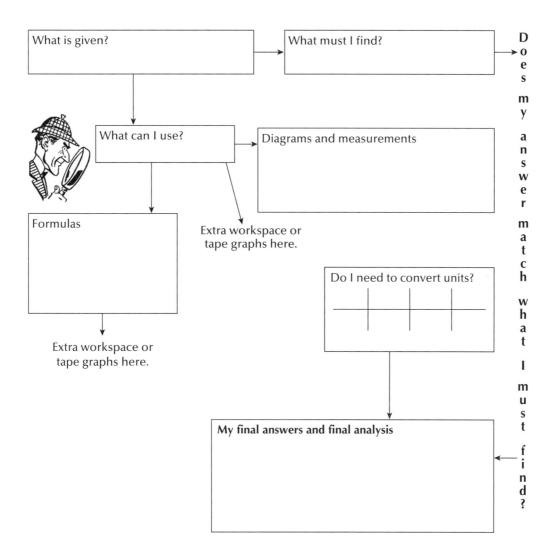

What is given?

What must I find?

What can I use?

Diagrams and measurements

Formulas

Extra workspace or tape graphs here.

Extra workspace or tape graphs here.

Do I need to convert units?

My final answers and final analysis

Does my answer match what I must find?

Lesson 14

RAINBOW PARABOLA

Level: For algebra students (enrichment: math)

Purpose: To discover the changes in parabolas using quadratic equations in the factored form; to create a familiar design with quadratic equations

Time: About 35 to 50 minutes

Materials: Graphing calculators; teacher and student copies of directions; graph paper; colored pencils

Procedure:

1. Distribute copies of directions or display them with an instructor's overhead calculator.

2. Follow the directions to create a rainbow.

3. Allow students to discover the changes that occur as they change numbers and window settings in the calculator.

4. Allow time for discussion and problem solving.

5. Challenge students to graph the rainbow on graph paper. Students will discover that the rainbow graphed on paper will be very steep unless they make adjustments to the units. *They should use a pencil before adding color.*

Evaluation: Rainbow Parabola is a fun way to review quadratic equations. Students can discuss the roots, solutions, and *x*-intercepts of quadratic equations in a factored form. It is an activity that focuses students on math used in different ways.

MAKING A RAINBOW WITH TI-83 OR TI-84 CALCULATOR

Steps	Press	Screen Displays
Step 1: clear the calculator.	2ND + 7 enter 1 2 RESET	RAM cleared
Step 2: check the axis	Zoom 6 or GRAPH	x,y axis
Step 3: enter a positive quadratic equation	Y1 = (X + 3) (X − 3) GRAPH	positive quadratic (a smile)
Step 4: flip the quadratic by inserting a negative in front of the first parentheses	Y1 = (−) (X + 3) (X − 3) GRAPH	negative quadratic (a frown)
Step 5: enter 3 more quadratic equations	Y2 = (−) (X + 2) (X − 2) GRAPH Y3 = (−) (X + 1) (X − 1) GRAPH Y4 = (−) (X + 0.5) (X − 0.5) GRAPH	four quadratic equations
Step 6: hide the axis	2ND ZOOM AXES OFF ENTER GRAPH	a rainbow
Step 7: change the window to make the rainbow wider	WINDOW set × min −6 × max 6 ENTER GRAPH	a better rainbow
Step 8: Students add a few more equations to make a larger rainbow and discover what numbers work best.		

To plot on graph paper and color the rainbow, students should deselect all graphs by pressing Y₁= and moving the cursor to the = mark. It will blink. Press ENTER to deselect the equation. Continue until all equations are deselected.

Pressing ENTER on the = again will allow the calculator to graph each equation separately. When the = sign is black, press 2ND GRAPH. A table of values for the selected equation will appear.

To avoid student errors in graphing, students should be shown the following key strokes:

XTθn key enters the variable X
Negative is the key with (−)
Subtraction is −

MATH LESSONS:
Algebra

Lesson 15
THE THROW DOWN

Level: Can be adapted for many levels (problem solving: all subjects)

Purpose: To introduce a new lesson and complete a note-taking chart

Time: About 20 minutes

Materials:

- Textbook
- Writing utensils; The Throw Down worksheet for group points
- Soft ball to toss around
- Timer (optional)

Procedure:

1. Decide on group or individual points and tell the class how they will earn points. The group or individuals with the most points wins the "Throw Down." *Choose a simple reward,* such as being the first students to leave the room, receiving a piece of candy from reward box, or gaining bonus points on a quiz. Awarding one to two points on a quiz to each member of the group with the most participation usually increases participation and more retention of information.

2. Students open textbooks to assigned lesson. For 5 to 7 minutes, the students read the text and take notes in their notebooks or on the note-taking chart. The notes may include definitions, key points, word problems, and strategies.

3. For group points, allow students 3 additional minutes on a timer to share notes. During the 3 minutes:

   They can highlight key notes.

   They rank the difficulty or importance of the information given.

   They do not spend time copying someone's notes.

4. For individual points, begin the toss.

5. The ball is tossed out by the teacher each turn to ensure that each group gets a chance. Each student who catches the ball reads one of his notes to the group. The teacher quickly records the note on the worksheet on the overhead projector or interactive board.

6. Student tosses the ball back and the teacher tosses to the next group or student. This continues until the chart is filled or material is covered. If one group does not have anything new to contribute to the chart, the next team gets a chance. A student can always defer to a teammate if he knows a partner has a more competitive concept or someone else used his note.

7. Each group is given 1 minute to discuss notes and vote for the Throw Down winner or winners. Points are recorded and prizes awarded. Teacher has the privilege of override and awarding points, too.

8. Students are given assignment to complete, may copy notes, or teacher may save notes and provide them through e-mail or technology linking home and school.

Evaluation: Throw Down is used when introducing a new skill. Throw Down is an interactive activity. Students have a chance to discuss procedures before beginning practice or seat work. It works very well when students will be working problems that combine several new steps or concepts, such as equations with variables on two sides or dividing mixed numbers.

It is also helpful before a quiz as a stress-relieving review.

Name: _____

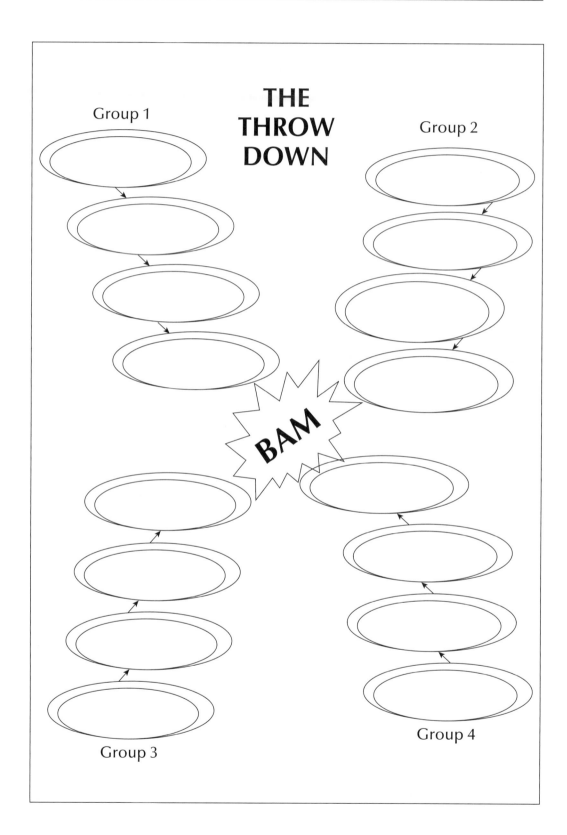

MATH LESSONS: Algebra

MATH LESSONS:
Algebra

Sample of teacher notes
Groups 2 and 4 are awarded
the points.

Lesson 2.1 Algebra,
McDougal-Littel Real # Line
9/16/07

THE THROW DOWN

Group 1

You can order # on a # line

We have real # in the book

< or > compares # -5 < -4

Pass

Group 2

Positive # to the right or "0"

You can plot points on a number line

Weather forecasters use negative and positive numbers

Velocity in negative and positive velocity = -10 ft per sec. going down

BAM

The scale marks are for integers

Real # are positive, zero, and negative on the number line

-|-8| = -8 keep negative on outside of | | symbol.

Pass

Group 3

Fractions are ok 1/2 is between "0" and "1" on right side of "0"

absolute value is the number of spaces from zero |3| = 3 |-3| = 3

-3 is opposite of 3

Velocity and speed are written differently -10 is velocity down |-10| = 10 ft/sec is the speed.

Group 4

Teachers notes

is symbol of "numbers".
< is lesser than
> is greater than
|8| is read absolute value of 8.

Lesson 16

BLACKBEARD'S CHALLENGE

Level: For fifth grade and up (enrichment: math, history)

Purpose: To plot points on a line in the coordinate plane

Time: 30 minutes

Materials:

- Map of trade triangle for class projection
- Worksheet
- Paper; pencils

Procedure:

1. Give students copies of map, and make sure that the map is also displayed on an overhead projector or an interactive whiteboard.

2. Tell students that they have 5 to 10 minutes to find and record 10 coordinate points that they think are on the trade route lines on the map.

3. Students volunteer coordinate pairs; teacher or students plot the points. If the points are on a trade route line, the students who volunteer that point have captured a ship. Many students enjoy accumulating team points.

4. Students can plot everyone's points. Students like to draw the Jolly Roger head and crossed bones or ships to mark the correct coordinate points.

5. The students can take the maps to social studies class. There is lots of information on the Internet on the social studies component of trade routes during the colonial period.

Evaluation: Blackbeard's Challenge is an interactive, cross-curricular lesson for reviewing the coordinate plane. Using an overhead or interactive board makes it fun for active learners. They enjoy activities containing movement and challenges.

Gotta name, mate?

This is a map of the Trade Triangle during the colonial period of the United States. You are Blackbeard trying to capture the trade ships. Find the (x,y) pairs that are on the trade route lines. Record your points in the chart. With your teacher, plot your coordinate points on the class chart. If your coordinates are correct, you will capture a ship on the trade route.

(x, y) Pairs

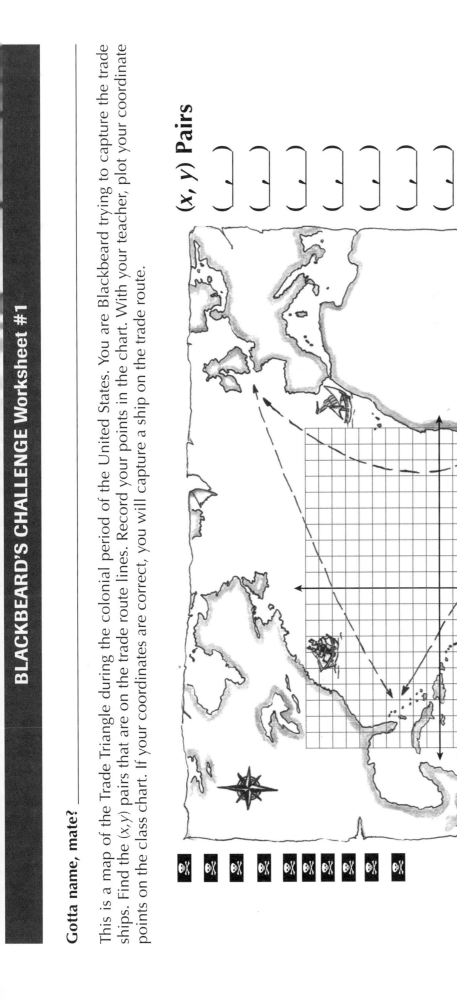

Map reprinted with the permission of the creator, Andrea Byrns.

ANSWERS TO BLACKBEARD'S CHALLENGE

This is a map of the Trade Triangle during the colonial period of the United States. You are a pirate trying to capture the trade ships. Work out the equations in the tables on the next 3 slides. With your teacher plot your coordinate points. If your math is correct, you will capture a ship on the trade route.

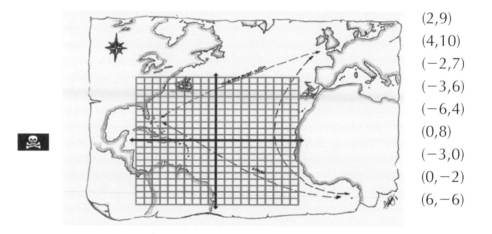

(2,9)
(4,10)
(−2,7)
(−3,6)
(−6,4)
(0,8)
(−3,0)
(0,−2)
(6,−6)

$$y = \frac{1}{2}x + 8$$

x	y
2	9
4	10
−2	7

$$y = \frac{2}{3}x + 8$$

x	y
−3	6
−6	4
0	8

$$y = -\frac{2}{3}x - 2$$

x	y
−3	0
0	−2
6	−6

Map reprinted with the permission of the creator, Andrea Byrns.

MATH LESSONS: Geometry

Lesson 17

HEAVENS TO BETSY: DESIGN YOUR OWN FLAG PROJECT

Level: Several levels for students fourth grade and up (enrichment: math, history)

Purpose: To identify and measure corresponding angles, alternate interior angles, and alternate exterior angles, and determine which angles are congruent to each other; to explore various triangle properties, such as scalene, isosceles, equilateral, acute, right, and obtuse; to write the equations of lines; to explore the history of the United States flag, good and bad flag designs, and create a personal flag using technology

Time: Several 30-minute periods for students to research various flags and their meanings; Several 30-minute periods to design the flag; and at least one 60-minute period to complete a finished drawing and produce accompanying information

Materials:

- Geometer's Sketchpad, or students can use the draw features of Microsoft Word, Microsoft Publisher, or KidPix to create their flags
- Without technology, use graph paper, rulers, compasses, protractors, colored pencils and markers

Procedure:

Geometry students

1. Complete the Good Flag, Bad Flag worksheet.

2. Sketch your drawing on a piece of paper before starting the drawing on sketchpad. You may change it as you see the lines and angles produced. Begin the technology-based or graph paper drawing. *Apply the ideas from a good flag design . . . don't get too fancy.*

You will need *two* copies of your flag.

1. One *without* measures and labels, to be colored for display.

2. One *with ALL* of the following:
   a. Every vertex labeled
   b. Every angle measured
   c. The equation of every line listed up in the left-hand corner
   d. The properties of every triangle identified, such as scalene, isosceles, equilateral, acute, right, and obtuse (you may have other shapes that can be identified)
   e. Corresponding angles, alternate interior angles, and alternate exterior angles identified and measured
   f. Congruent angles identified.

Algebra 1 and geometry students

Have fun being creative. The flags will be displayed on Veteran's Day with *outstanding* designs to represent how great students like you can apply the algebra and geometry skills. Your work will be graded and your flags judged by some local historians! Prizes will be awarded.

Extra: Collaborate with the language arts teachers. Students can read poems or other works about flags, pointing out references to what has been covered in this lesson.

Evaluation: This is best used after paper-and-pencil identification lessons on angles and parallel lines. Basic learners identify positions in transversals. Proficient to advanced learners should be able to name the following angle relationships: Alternate interior angles, alternate exteriors angles, vertical angles and corresponding angles are equal. Consecutive interior angles and all other pairs formed by one transversal and two parallel lines are supplementary.

GOOD AND BAD FLAG DESIGN Worksheet

Name:_____

Directions: Use the following website to complete the worksheet. Do this activity before you begin making your original flag.

http://www.nava.org/Flag%20Design/GFBF/index.html

1. What is the study of flags called? _____

2. Draw and label the anatomy of a flag.

3. List and describe the five basic principles of design of a flag.

   (1)

   (2)

   (3)

   (4)

   (5)

4. Using the principle of *Keep It Simple,* compare and contrast the Congo and West Virginia flags.

5. What makes the flags of Bangladesh and Alaska easy to remember (see page 5)?

6. What is the importance of symbolism in a flag (see page 6)?

7. What do the parallel lines and colors in the flags of Italy and the Ukraine symbolize (see page 7)?

8. What makes the OAS flag a difficult pattern (see page 7)?

9. What are the key concepts about the use of color in a flag? What does it mean "to reproduce in grayscale" (see page 8)?

10. Why is Virginia's flag considered a bad flag design (see page 9)?

11. Why are seals and words difficult to use in flags? According to these principles, does your state flag have a good design? Do you agree or disagree? Why?

12. Look at page 11 for only two seconds. Without looking again, try to reproduce the flag in the left top corner on the back of this page. Write the names of the colors you remember.

13. How is the flag of Ghana related to other flags in Africa? Why does the South Carolina flag look good hanging beside the United States flag?

14. Which flag do you like on page 13 and why?

15. Page 14 refers to width and length ratios: 1:1.5 or 1:2. Some good ratios are: 2 × 4, 4 × 6, and 8 × 12. When you design you flag try to use the above ratios. State three other things you might consider in designing your flag (from page 14).

16. Now for a *quick test*, study the flags on page 15 for about 20 seconds. Look away and see which ones you can draw from memory.

HEAVENS TO BETSY, WHO IS ROBERT G. HEFT?

Name: _____

Date: _____

Robert G. Heft was a young man when he suggested important changes to our flag. Go the website below and find 13 interesting facts about Robert G. Heft. Record your answers in complete sentences. Check your grammar and punctuation with a partner before you turn in the work.

◊ http://www.ideafinder.com/features/everwonder/won-flag.htm

1. _____

2. _____

3. _____

4. _____

5. _____

6. _____

7. _____

8. _____

9. _____

10. _____

11. _____

12. _____

13. _____

Lesson 18
PARALLEL PLAY: EQUAL OR SUPPLEMENTARY

Level: For algebra level and above (enrichment: math)

Purpose: To review and identify angle relationships in parallel lines with a transversal

Time: 20 minutes

Materials:

- Two different colors of "sidewalk" chalk (preferably green and blue) *or* about 35 feet of rope cut into three pieces. (One piece is 20 feet long, and the other two pieces are about 7 feet long. Blue, yellow, or green rope works well.)
- Pen or pencil with chart for group points if awarding team points.
- A soft, easy-to-catch ball to toss around.
- A sunny day or a large space indoors.

Procedure:

1. Go outside. Draw the transversal and two parallel lines on the concrete or place the 3 ropes down to make a transversal and parallel lines. See worksheet. Tell the students which is the top and bottom of the area. (Important: Putting the ropes down is quicker and easy to replace as students move ropes with their feet. Students might trip if ropes are anchored in place with books, so just relax and let the students put them back in place if moved. Chalk is safer but not always allowed.)

2. Students stand in a line around the outside of the parallel lines so they can see. For team competition, separate teams on different sides of the transversal facing each other.

3. The first student comes out and stands between the parallel lines. The teacher tosses the ball up. The student moves, catches the ball, and goes to the nearest angle to stand. He calls out one of the following positions: "above a parallel line, on the exterior," "below a parallel line, on the exterior," "above a parallel line, on the interior," or "below a parallel line, on the interior." He holds the ball and waits for the next student.

4. The next student or a team member comes out and stands between the parallel lines. The previous student tosses the ball up. The new student moves, catches the ball, and goes to the nearest angle to stand. He calls out one of the following positions: "above a parallel line, on the exterior," "below a parallel line, on the exterior," "above a parallel line, on the interior," or "below a parallel line, on the interior," and adds "same side (or different side) of the transversal" (as the other student).

5. For whole-class participation, the teacher can call on a volunteer to name the relationship of the two angles.

6. For team competition, the two players must identify the relationship between the angles they are standing in and tell the teacher. If correct they get the points. Student tosses the ball back to the teacher to begin a new round. The new students follow the same pattern of play from steps 3 and 4 until all students have had a turn.

Evaluation: This is best used after paper-and-pencil identification lessons on angles and parallel lines. Basic learners identify positions in transversals. Proficient to advanced learners should be able to name the following angle relationships: Alternate interior angles, alternate exterior angles, vertical angles and corresponding angles are equal to one another. Consecutive interior angles and all other pairs of one transversal and two parallel lines are supplementary to one another.

PARALLEL PLAY Worksheet

Name: _____

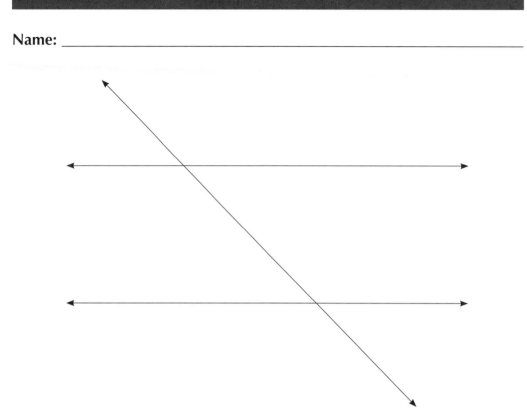

Corresponding Angles	Corresponding Angles	Alternate Exterior Angles	Alternate Exterior Angles	Alternate Interior Angles
Alternate Interior Angles	Vertical Angles	Vertical Angles	Transversal	Parallel Line
Parallel Line	Consecutive Interior Angles	Consecutive Interior Angles		

Lesson 19

SCALE MODELS

Level: For beginning level students working with ratio and proportion (enrichment: math)

Purpose: To familiarize students with linear measurement, calculating area, and working with ratio and proportion

Time: About 30 minutes on each of two days

Materials:

- 12-inch ruler; worksheet
- Graph paper with 1/4" rule

Procedure:

First day:

1. Distribute rulers and first worksheet.

2. Have students measure the first line and then calculate what it would be in a model drawn to 1/4 inch scale (in which 1/4 inch equals 1 foot). They should draw that line and place it next to 1(b).

3. Have students measure the rectangle and write the values for length, width, and area on the appropriate lines.

4. Have students calculate a 1/4 inch-scale model of the rectangle and draw it in the space at 2(b), writing the values for length, width, and area on the appropriate lines.

5. Students will write the areas of the two figures in the appropriate places and calculate the ratio of the areas.

6. Have students talk generally about models. What do they know about the ratios of model cars and airplanes? What is the ratio between blueprints and the full sized building?

7. Homework: students are to identify a room either at home or at school and measure the dimensions. Discuss why the room should not be larger than 32 feet by 44 feet if it is to be drawn on a graph that is 8 inches by 11 inches.

Second day:

1. Students will write down the dimensions of the room they have chosen and calculate what the dimensions of the ¼ inch model will be. Talk about the problems of drawing models when the original dimensions may have inches and parts of inches.

2. Distribute graph paper and have students draw on it a scale drawing of the room they have selected. Make sure that students label each line as to its original dimension and its model dimension.

3. Either have students bring in scale models of objects or provide scale models for students to figure out what the original size of the objects was. Hot Wheels are either 1:64 for standard cars or 1:43 for slightly larger models. Matchbox cars vary and can be 1:100 scale, 1:64 scale, or 1:43 scale. Provide models for which the original dimensions can be located easily (usually on the Internet) to enable students to compare the relative sizes.

Evaluation: Ratio and proportion is a topic many students find difficult. Having real objects to compare helps students see the connection between the original size and the reduced model size.

SCALE MODEL Worksheet

Name: _____

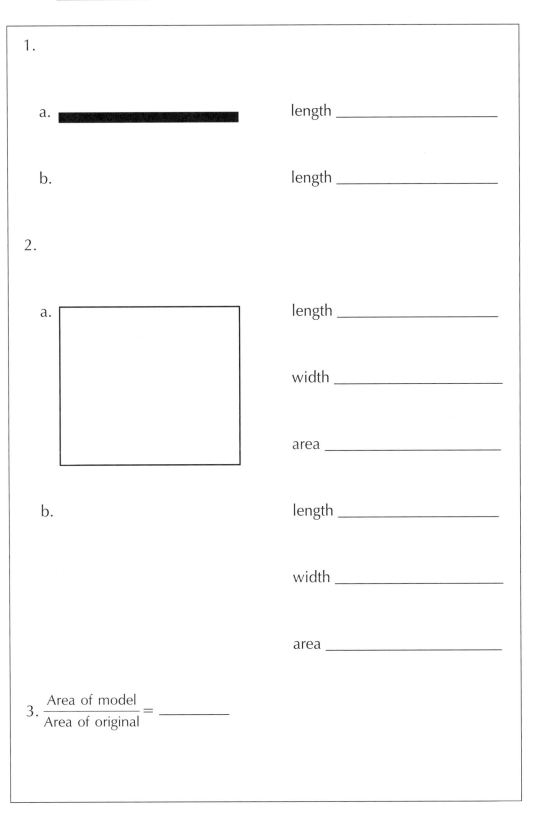

1.

   a.   ▬▬▬▬▬▬▬▬▬   length _____

   b.   length _____

2.

   a.   ☐   length _____

                               width _____

                               area _____

   b.   length _____

                               width _____

                               area _____

3. $\dfrac{\text{Area of model}}{\text{Area of original}} =$ _____

Lesson 20

THE COVER-UP: A PAINT DILEMMA

Topic: For students familiar with ratio and proportion (enrichment: math, science, economics)

Purpose:

> To compute surface area of various shapes using a real-life model (a birdhouse)

> To convert units of measure expressed in inches, feet, quarts, and gallons

Time: About 50 minutes

Materials:

- Purchased or student-made birdhouses
- Writing utensils; rulers and protractors; calculators (optional)
- Chart from Problem Solving with Holmes (Lesson 13 in this chapter)
- 3 quarts of paint for the birdhouses; paintbrushes

Procedure:

1. Individual students or partners are given a student-made or purchased birdhouse.

2. Students are given the following paint dilemma word problem.

   The students made 26 (or some other total) birdhouses. The parents purchased 3 quarts of paint. Calculate the surface area of your birdhouse in square inches. The can of paint says that 1 gallon should cover 400 square feet of area.

   Will 3 quarts be enough for the class to paint the birdhouses? Justify your answer.

3. Students draw a diagram of each side of the birdhouse, measure in inches and label the drawings on the Holmes chart. Depending on student level with fraction computations, students may use rounding skills to make the math easier.

4. Students use their textbooks or are given formulas for each shape.

5. Students compute and total the outside surface area of the birdhouse.

6. Do the conversions. This is the most difficult step and missed by even the best math students. The students will have various methods of converting units. The error occurs when dividing by the square unit. The students convert from square inches to square feet by dividing by 144. 1 square foot = 144 square inches. (*The students will want to divide only by 12 and miss the squaring part.*)

7. Students total the class answers on the board or overhead projector.

8. Convert again: Students must realize that a quart of paint is only 100 square feet. (The word problem says that a gallon is 400 square feet.) Students then decide if the 3 quarts of paint will cover the birdhouses.

Evaluation: The paint dilemma is a highly engaging, hands-on, authentic task. It requires students to apply formulas and use measuring skills. It is adjusted to the level of proficiency students have with multiplication and division of fractions. Discuss that estimation by rounding fractions is fine because painting is not an exact procedure due to waste and brush sizes.

This is an excellent culminating activity for a state exam requirement of computing surface area. It makes an engaging geometry project. The birdhouses can be painted and donated for a cross-curricular service learning project.

Lesson 21a

MAKING ROCKET CANDY

Topic: Basic level fourth grade and up (enrichment: math, science)

Purpose: To apply formulas of volume to geometric solids; to use candy rocket design to engage learners in a lesson that can be cross-curricular

Time: 60 minutes (you will need to build an example, and that will take some time on your own)

Materials:

- Beginning level students: Worksheet Activity 1
- Candy for students: Starbursts (three per student), Smarties (three per student), and a Hershey's Kiss
- 3-by-4-inch piece of paper; several rolls of transparent tape; metric rulers

Procedure:

Beginning Level Activity 1

1. Introduce the lesson. Read selection from *Rocket Boys* by Homer Hickam. Suggested passages are those where the boys try to figure out how to build a rocket.

2. Tell students that they are going to build a candy rocket, show them your example rocket, and pass out candy.

3. Discuss the general shape of the pieces of candy. Ask students to recall the formulas for the volume of a cylinder, a rectangular prism, and a cone.

4. Give out the worksheet and the centimeter rulers. Ask students to describe how to get the different measurements needed for each piece of candy.

5. Review measuring in centimeters if your class is weak in decimals.

6. With a partner, students measure and record their data on the worksheet for the Smarties.

7. Students should have their measurements checked by the teacher and then start on the volume formula.

8. Teacher checks the values calculated for the volume of a Smartie. If correct, students may tape the candies together (see Illustration 1) and cut out a 3-by-4-inch piece of paper to tape around and decorate.

9. Discuss the difference between slant height and height inside the Hershey's Kiss. Show the students a Kiss cut in half, and measure it in front of the class.

10. With a partner, students measure and record their data on the worksheet for the Hershey's Kiss.

MATH LESSONS: Geometry

11. Students should have their measurements checked by the teacher, then start on the volume formula.

12. Students tape the Kiss to the top of the decorated rocket.

13. With a partner, students measure and record their data on the worksheet for the Starbursts.

14. Students should have their measurements checked by the teacher and then start on the volume formula. They must multiply by the number of Starbursts to record the total volume.

15. Students balance rockets on Starbursts and turn in their worksheets.

Evaluation: Students enjoy the challenge of measuring the candy and designing their rocket. It is an engaging way to practice a routine seatwork task of practicing formulas.

ROCKET CANDY Worksheet, Activity # 1

Name: _____

MATH LESSONS:
Geometry

STEP 1: MEASURE THE CANDY (Use a metric ruler and round centimeters to nearest tenth)	Step 2: COMPUTE THE VOLUME (Round answers to nearest tenth.)
Starbursts rectangular prism platform	**V = s²h or V = lwh**
Square sides (length × width): _____cm	
Height : _____cm	
	Volume: _____ cm³
	Multiply by the number of Starbursts
	Total volume: _____ cm³
Smarties cylinder fuel	**V = h(πr²)**
Diameter of one Smarties: _____cm	
Radius of one Smarties: _____cm	
Height or length of Smarties: _____cm	
	Volume: _____cm³
	Multiply by 3
	Total volume: _____ cm³
Hershey's Kiss cone spaceship	**V= 1/ 3 h (πr²)**
Diameter of the base: _____cm	
Radius of the base: _____cm	
Height*: _____cm	
	Volume:_____ cm³
	Volume of all Starbursts: _____ cm³
	Volume of Hershey's Kiss: _____ cm³
	Volume of Starbursts: _____cm³
	Total volume of rocket: _____ cm³

* Cross-section of the Hershey's Kiss

Lesson 21b

MAKING ROCKET CANDY

Topic: For proficient to advanced students (enrichment: math, science)

Purpose: To apply formulas of volume to geometric solids; to use candy rocket design to engage learners in a lesson that can be cross-curricular

Time: 60 minutes

Materials:

- Activity 2 worksheet
- Candy for students: Miniature Reese's Peanut Butter Cups (three per student), Smarties (three per student), a Hershey Kiss, one Wint-O-Green mint
- A 3-by-4-inch piece of paper; several rolls of transparent tape; metric rulers

Procedure:

1. Introduce the lesson. Read selection from *Rocket Boys* by Homer Hickam.

2. Tell students that they are going to build a candy rocket and show them your sample.

3. Pass out the candy only.

4. Discuss the general shape of the pieces of candy. Ask students to recall the formulas for volume of cylinders and a cone. Introduce the circular frustum as a new geometric solid. Explain that it is part of a cone. A student should discover that the Hershey's Kiss and Reese's Peanut Butter Cup fit together to make a cone. (Some will say it looks like an elephant's stand.)

5. Give out the worksheet and the centimeter rulers. The formulas for the Wint-O-Green mint, Hershey's Kiss, and Reese's Peanut Butter Cup will require more mathematical reasoning from the students. The following teacher notes and pictures will help.

   Ask students to describe how to get the different measurements needed for each piece of candy following the order of the chart. Advise them that we are making our best estimate of the candy's dimensions. To obtain the radii, they will be measuring the diameters in centimeters, then dividing the values in half.
   The Smarties should be easy for advanced students. The Wint-O-Green requires that the volume of the hole be subtracted from the overall volume of the mint as a cylinder. Ask students to first compute the volume of the hole, then the volume of the complete mint, then subtract the first value from the second value. Then using the same

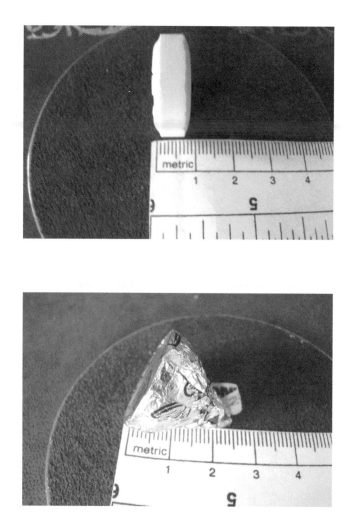

radii, ask students to compute using the formula on the worksheet. Caution the students to be careful with the squaring of the radii. Some students may argue that there is enough mint in the roundness of the sides that you don't need to take out the volume of the hole. As a class you may decide to make that adjustment and just use the volume of a cylinder for the mint using the total radius.

The Hershey's Kiss requires the students to get a hidden height inside the cone. If they are stumped, draw a cross-section of the Kiss and see if anyone suggests using the Pythagorean theorem. The slant height is c, the hypotenuse. The radius is b. The height will be a. So $c^2 - b^2 = a^2$ and you have the height.

In the frustum, students will need the hidden height also. To measure that without cutting, students can simply place a ruler on the upper base or top, line it up with a wall or board on the desk, and mark the height, mimicking the same procedure as when they get their height by standing against the wall. Another option is using the Pythagorean theorem to find the value for a, the height of the triangle. Put the Kiss on top of the Reese's Peanut Butter Cup. Find the slant height c of total cone. Find the radius of the bottom of the Reese's Peanut Butter Cup for b. When students have the height of the total cone, they subtract the height from the height in the Hershey's Kiss problem to obtain the remaining height of the frustum.

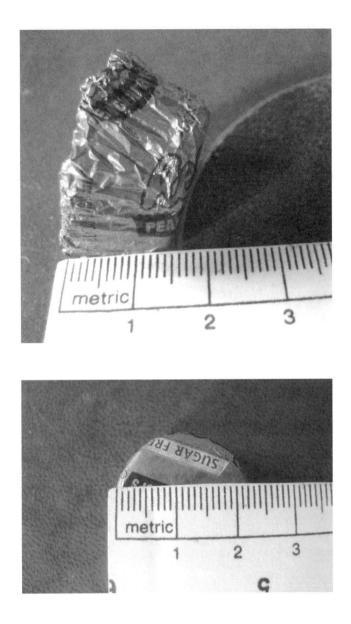

6. Students should have their measurements checked by the teacher and then start on the volume formulas.

7. To assemble the rockets:
   a. Tape together three Smarties. Tape the Wint-O-Green o-ring to the bottom.
   b. Cut out a 3-by-4-inch piece of paper to tape around and decorate.
   c. Students tape the Kiss to the top of the decorated rocket.

8. Students balance rockets on Reese's Peanut Butter Cup and turn in their worksheets.

Evaluation: Students enjoy the challenge of measuring the candy and designing their rocket. It is an engaging way to practice a usual seatwork task of practicing formulas.

ROCKET CANDY Worksheet, Activity 2

Name: _____

STEP 1: MEASURE THE CANDY (Round centimeters to nearest tenth)	Step 2: COMPUTE THE VOLUME (Round answers to nearest tenth)
Smarties cylinder fuel	$V = h(\pi r^2)$
Diameter of one Smartie = _____ cm	
Radius of one Smartie = _____ cm	
Height or length of Smartie = _____ cm	V = _____ cm^3
	Multiply by three Smarties
	Total V = _____ cm^3
Wint-O-Green cylinder O-ring	$V = h(\pi)(R^2 - r^2)$
Diameter of total mint = _____ cm	
Radius of total mint (R) = _____ cm	
Diameter of center/hole = _____ cm	
Radius of center/hole (r) = _____ cm	
Height of mint = _____ cm	V = _____ cm^3
Hershey's Kiss cone spaceship	$V = 1/3\, h\,(\pi r^2)$
Diameter of the base = _____ cm	
Radius of the base = _____ cm	
Slant Height = _____ cm	
Height = _____ cm	V = _____ cm^3
Frustum or Reese's Peanut Butter Cup launchers	$V = 1/3 \pi h\,(R^2 + Rr + r^2)$
Diameter of lower base = _____ cm	
Radius of lower base (R) = _____ cm	
Diameter of upper base = _____ cm	
Radius of upper base (r) = _____ cm	
Height = _____ cm	V = _____ cm^3

	Volume of three Smarties = _____ cm³
	Volume of Wint-O-Green = _____ cm³
	Volume of Hershey's Kiss = _____ cm³
	Volume of Reese's Peanut Butter Cup = _____ cm³
	Total volume of rocket = _____ cm³

3

Language Arts

Writing is far more complicated than just putting words on the page. To begin with, the writer has to have some form of organization so that what is written is coherent, purposeful, and understandable. In a science class taught by one of the authors of this book, a student was having trouble writing a lab report. She liked to write, but the structure of a lab report was very limiting for her, and what she produced was more like the story of a lab rather than the report of a lab exercise. The teacher used a form of the Constructing Language lesson (Lesson 36 in this book) and had her write each step and result from the lab on an index card. Then she arranged the cards in the most logical order, so that each step followed the one before it. Once she saw the correct order, she was better able to write the report. Even with this structure, she still had trouble with the discussion section. Once she realized that the discussion followed from the results, she would remove each result card as she incorporated that information in the discussion. That method kept her from repeating herself as she discussed the findings in the lab exercise.

Generally, the students who have trouble with writing are boys, but in this case, a student with excellent writing skills found it difficult to produce a structured report. There are different types of writing, and students who are good at one form may find it difficult to excel at another type. One of us has the opposite problem from this student and found reports much easier to write than narrative pieces. We found that it helped to use the same process—putting the parts of the story together—that was being creating on cards. That method provided the structure that was needed to create the narrative.

At least part of the trouble with writing for boys is thought to be caused by poor handwriting (Graham, Harris, & Fink, 2000). There are several explanations for why boys are more likely to have poor handwriting. They are slower to acquire fine motor skills than girls, and their verbal skills tend to develop more slowly (Graham, Berninger, Weintraub, & Schafer, 1998; Medwell & Wray, 2008). Handwriting problems have been linked with spelling problems and difficulties in verbal expression, both of which result in the production of poor writing (Montgomery, 2008).

An additional problem with handwriting is *dysgraphia* or *dyspraxia,* which is identified in boys more often than in girls. This disorder is sometimes known as Developmental Coordination Disorder (DCD) and is the result of poor fine motor coordination (Montgomery, 2008). Individuals with DCD find the act of writing tiring and have difficulty writing for long. They cannot form letters correctly, cannot write on a straight line, and cannot write fast enough to keep up with what a teacher is saying. This is a particular problem on timed writing tests or any test which requires free-response answers. One of us is a fellow sufferer and can attest to the difficulty the individual with dysgraphia has in transferring words from one's imagination to the page. Technology is a great help, and without a computer it would be impossible for her to write these words. In particular, spelling is a problem connected with dysgraphia, and without the spell-check feature, you would not be able to read what has been written here. Of course, there are times when her spelling is so wrong that even spell-check cannot figure out what word she wants, and then we are all grateful for the thesaurus feature of her word processing program.

The active learner can find writing an easier task than reading, which is more passive. Strange as it may seem, getting a poor reader to begin to write will frequently assist his reading skills. Several of the lessons in this section are designed to help students learn to write without requiring them to actually put pen (or pencil) to paper. Getting students to start the process of sorting through ideas and putting them in order will start them on the road to writing. While the author who suffers from dysgraphia found it almost impossible to write an essay in school, she was a whiz at lab reports. When her English teacher found that out, the teacher showed her how to structure her essays so that they were easier for her to write. She says that she will never write a novel, but she can put her thoughts and ideas on the page in a clear and coherent fashion so that others can know what she is thinking.

Reading is a problem for many boys around the world (U.S. Department of Education, 2008; U.K. Department for Education, 2009). One theory is that the reason for boys' poor reading skills is due to the slower development of the left side of the brain, where the verbal center begins (Halpern, 2000; Kimura, 2000). Another consideration is that parents talk more to girls than to boys, with the result that girls are more ready for school than are boys, particularly in verbal and reading areas (Whitehead, 2006).

Yet another issue for boys in school is that their emotional response to the course or to the teacher makes a huge difference in how well they do (Freudenthaler, Spinath, & Neubauer, 2008; Koepke & Harkins, 2008). When they like the subject, they work hard; when they don't, they won't work. And the same is true when they like the teacher or if they think the teacher doesn't like them. Additionally, their emotional involvement in a class is increased if their peer group is also involved (Vande Gaer, Pustjens, Van Damme, & De Munter, 2007). Some of the lessons in the reading section of this chapter are designed to get students excited about or involved with what they will be reading.

What are some of the other reasons that a child might have trouble with language based classes?

1. *Dyslexia:* This is a general term for several different disorders involving problems with reading, writing, or understanding language. The severity can be so mild that the individual may not even be aware of any difficulties, or can be so severe that the individual will require assistance and special training to function in school. It is important to remember that dyslexia is primarily a problem in school (or wherever the individual is required to use written language). In many settings, the individual with dyslexia functions entirely normally. Children who have been diagnosed with a form of dyslexia can get the impression that they are unable to learn anything, but that is not true. If the dyslexia involves problems with spoken language, that may have a greater impact on the individual, but for many activities language is not required, and the individual will function normally. For the dyslexic student, a more active approach to learning will help that student have a better chance of reaching academic goals. And, while most students who are identified with dyslexia are boys, girls who are identified with one of the varieties of dyslexia tend to have much more serious problems than most boys. Active learning will give them a way to learn that suits their learning strengths.

   a. *Differential laterality:* We have already noted that the left side of the brain is the area in which the language center begins and that area of the brain develops first in girls (Schmithorst, Holland, & Dardzinski, 2008; Shucard & Shucard, 1990). For many boys, that means that they enter school less fluent in verbal skills, and that may seem to be a form of dyslexia. If care is taken to make sure that boys are exposed to verbal tasks, they will develop verbal skills; over time, their verbal deficits may be reduced or even eliminated.

   b. *Developmental Differences:* Is it dyslexia if the difference is due to development? It is by a strict definition of the term, but the difference is huge for the boy. If he thinks that his reading problems are due to a problem with the way his brain processes language, he may give up, but if he understands that the problem is developmental and that time and practice will help, he will be more willing to try, especially if the exercises are interesting and active.

2. *Vision:* When we look at any object, we are usually not aware that we are moving our eyes around to get a more complete picture. We only focus on a small area in the front of our field of vision, and if we did not move our eyes around we would find most of what we see rather fuzzy. Moving our eyes allows us to get a clearer picture of our world. When we

read, we tend to move our eyes laterally so that we can see briefly what is coming up. That gives us a better idea of what we are reading. If we only read one word at a time, we may not totally understand the meaning. Those eye movements are called *saccades* and are larger in novice readers and in boys (Bednarek et al., 2006; Joseph et al., 2008). An active approach to learning may well get the student engaged in a task, giving the student time to develop control of his eyes.

3. *Hearing:* There is some indication that young boys do not hear as well as girls do, perhaps due to a lack of sensitivity to sound (Boatella-Costa, Costas-Moragas, Mussons-Botet, Fornieles-Deu, & De Cáceres-Zurita, 2007). That may contribute to the observation that parents don't talk to sons (Whitehead, 2006), especially if the reason for the lack of conversation is that boys don't respond to parents because they either don't have the verbal skills or don't hear when parents speak softly. Whatever the reason, many teachers have observed that boys have trouble learning to read because they do not have good phonemic awareness (James, 2007).

If a child in your class is having trouble with verbal tasks, that problem may be due to learning disabilities, to disinterest, or to lack of exposure to language early in life. In addition, inactivity may interfere with a child remembering what is said, as very active children find it difficult to sit still when the teacher is talking and may miss much of what is said. The teacher wants the child to listen and believes that if the child is moving, the child is not paying attention, when the opposite may be true. There is some indication that movement on the part of boys actually may improve their memory (Rapport et al., 2009). When students are involved in an activity and the teacher needs to tell the students something, most teachers will ask the students to stop and pay attention to the message. It may be more effective for active learners simply to ask them to pay attention while they continue with the activity.

When boys are asked what lessons they find most interesting and from which they learn the most, they will list those that involve physical activity and active involvement (Reichart & Hawley, 2009). Active learners require activity and they learn best by doing, not listening.

Interactive language activities

- help students to become engaged in the lesson rather than just observe,
- provide an active rather than passive approach to language, and
- encourage students to attempt new skills.

Lesson 22
ANTICIPATION SLIDESHOW

Level: Can be adapted for many levels (incentive activity: language arts, history, science)

Purpose: Engaging some students in literacy and stimulating intrinsic motivation to read is a difficult task for teachers within the language arts classroom. Therefore, it is essential that active students be interested, intrigued, and curious about literature before the actual reading begins.

Time: 30 minutes

Materials: A collection of pictures and words extracted from an upcoming text (this collection can be arranged as a PowerPoint presentation, on a poster board, or as a collage)

Procedure: For this strategy, a collection of ambiguous pictures, words, and phrases are arranged in a PowerPoint slideshow; each picture, word, or phrase should be directly related to the text. However, it is important to choose a random selection of ideas from the novel or short story. The slideshow should not be predictable or easily comprehensible for students. After showing students the presentation, challenge students to make predictions about the text, using the cues *who, what, where, when,* and *why.*

1. Prior to the start of a novel or short story study, create a selection of PowerPoint slides that reveal different aspects of the literature (for example, pictures of characters, excerpts of dialogue, and descriptions of conflicts).

2. Show the slides to students; as they view, instruct students to begin predicting in order to answer the 5 *W*s about the novel (*who, what, where, why, when*).

3. After students have created a prediction about the novel or short story, allow each student an opportunity to share his ideas about the text.

Evaluation: Reward the student who creates a prediction that most closely matches the actual text; this will motivate other students to analyze and critique the slideshow clues the next time the strategy is utilized.

ANTICIPATION SLIDESHOW EXAMPLE FOR
JOHNNY TREMAIN

The following pictures and words would be projected onto a screen or board one at a time:

Silver

Tea

Rats

Red Coat

After each picture or word goes up, ask the students what they think the book is going to be about. By the time the last picture is displayed, the students should be able to figure out what era the book will be laid in. Once the students have finished reading the story, you could show them this list again and ask them how each item fits into the story. What would they have chosen instead?

Lesson 23
BOOKMARKS

Level: Can be adapted for many levels (incentive activity: language arts)

Purpose: Having a task to do will increase the chance that active learners will read. Finding a passage that matches the bookmark gives the students something to do. You can also require students to write the reason that they selected the passage and what it is about the selection that matches the bookmark. For older students, the bookmarks involve abstract ideas, and the justification may require a longer answer.

Time: It should not take you long to introduce your class to the idea of using the bookmarks. After that, each time students begin a new book, they can pick the bookmarks from a holder, or you can spread them face down on a desk for them to pick at random.

Materials: There are several sample bookmarks included on the next pages, but you can make your own using clip art from your computer. You will want to duplicate these onto stiff paper or card stock, but be careful if you laminate them because that will make them slick and they may slip out of the books.

Procedure: Introduce the notion of using the bookmarks.

1. Show the students the bookmarks and tell them what they are to do with them. Generally, each student selects three bookmarks and marks a page that matches the description or idea on each bookmark.

2. You can let the students select the bookmarks at random or let them choose which three they want.

3. This exercise can be done with assigned reading or with materials that they are reading on their own.

4. Remind students periodically that they should be finding passages in their reading materials that match their bookmarks. You can require students to copy down the passage that they feel best describes the bookmark. Older students might be asked to write a description of the passage that exemplifies the bookmark, explaining why they made the selection.

5. For younger children, you can display the selections together with the bookmark, and the students can discuss how well they think the selection reflects the message on the bookmark. Older students might debate the appropriateness of the selections, especially if several students receive identical bookmarks.

Evaluation: For younger children, simply selecting the passages is evidence that they used the bookmarks. Older children may be assessed through assigned papers, through participation in a debate, or in presenting their selections to the class.

BOOKMARKS (for younger students)

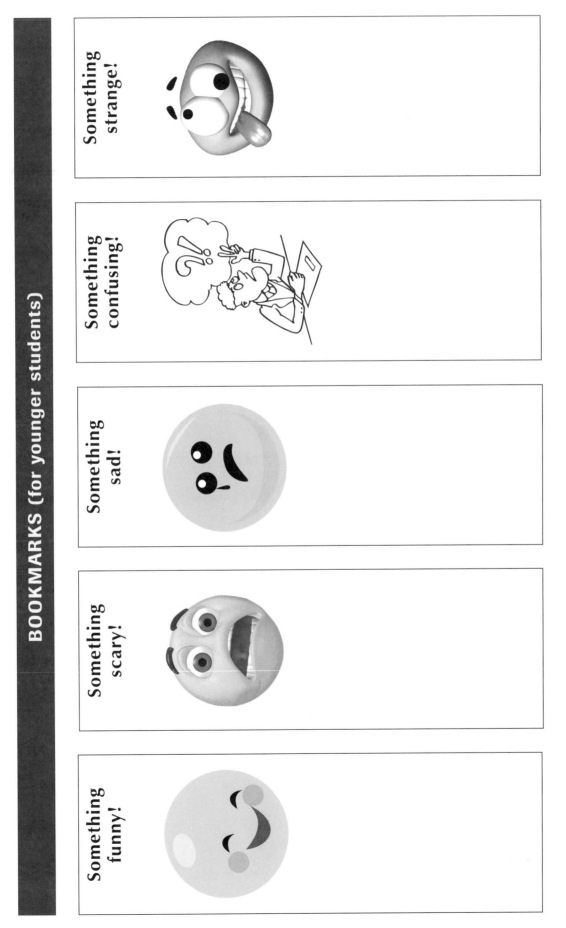

Something strange!

Something confusing!

Something sad!

Something scary!

Something funny!

BOOKMARKS (for older students)

This part of the story was a surprise!

Something I learned from the story

This part of the story could be left out

Theme of the story

Reason for title

Lesson 24
BRING-ME GAME

Level: For younger students (review: language arts, social studies, science, history)

Purpose: This strategy keeps active students in motion while they review material for class. The combination of physical motion with competition will help these students pay attention to the task at hand.

Time: 45 minutes

Materials: Content questions on sentence strips or index cards; a chair; pencils; a large area

Procedure:

1. Create several review questions based on previously studied content. Examples of such questions might be "What is a simile?" or "Write a sentence with two prepositional phrases." Make multiple copies of the questions, and cut them into individual strips or put them on index cards.

2. Sit in a chair in the center of the room. Have the students sit in pairs in a semicircle around you. Among each pair of students, one person is the designated "getter," while the other person is the designated "taker."

3. The "getter" runs to the chair, takes the question, and returns it to his or her partner; together, they write the answer to the question on the card or strip (or a small whiteboard, if you want to reuse the index cards). Then the "taker" runs it back to the game facilitator. A point is rewarded to each team who returns the correct answer.

   It is essential that each group is the same distance away from the chair. The game is most effective in a large area (for example, outside or in a multi-purpose room); however, it can be played inside the classroom if desks and chairs are pushed to the corners of the room.

Evaluation: If one team always answers the questions first, then award points for all correct answers. This helps to keep competition equal and encourages all students to stay engaged. This exercise is for review, and success in this activity is reflected in student engagement and achievement on conventional assessment activities.

Lesson 25
BUILDING THE SETTING

Level: For all levels (alternate modality: language arts, history, social studies)

Purpose: Because many active learners are iconic learners, remembering what they see better than what they read, building models of a scene in a story will help them recall details and events. In order to build the model correctly, the student has to find the passage or passages which refer specifically to the setting being built and include that reference in the model.

Time: Three 60-minute class periods

Materials: Shoeboxes; cardboard; glue, tape; scissors; markers; posterboard; index cards; toothpicks; clay; Internet access. (*Note:* Supplies may vary depending on the types of visual projects that students choose to create.)

Procedure:

1. This strategy allows students the opportunity to actively explore the importance of setting within literature as they recreate a model of a story's setting.

   a. After reading a text to the entire group, students choose one specific setting from the text (for example, the character's home, work place, or community) for which a visual, three-dimensional model can be built.

   b. After the scene has been selected, students should pick out at least three important visual details from the text that describe the setting. These passages should be recorded on three separate index cards.

   c. In order to complete this project, students may create dioramas, clay models, paintings, murals, photo essays, shadow boxes, or any other type of visual model.

   d. Within the setting model, students must label various structures that are explained in the text using index cards and toothpicks. For example, if the student is recreating the sidewalk setting from *The Giver* by Lois Lowry, she must find a passage of text that supports the inclusion of bicycles in the model. The passage can be recorded onto an index card and stuck into the model using toothpicks.

   e. To make the project more elaborate, require students to extract 8 to 10 visual details from the text that describe the setting.

2. Allow students at least two complete class periods to build their settings. All construction should occur within the classroom if students are working in pairs or small groups.

3. After students have completed the setting projects, display the models around the classroom with a small piece of numbered paper in front of each model. Each setting model should reflect a different scene from the shared text.

4. After students have completed the construction of the setting models, all students should participate in a gallery walk around the classroom. During the gallery walk, students examine their classmates' models, determine which scene is being reflected in the model, and write a brief plot synopsis of what occurred in the specific scene. This activity encourages students to closely examine a story's elements by combing the text for explicit details about setting and plot. For example, if a student creates a setting model of the playground in *The Giver*, the other students in the class are asked to examine the model, determine the specific scene that it represents, and write a brief summary of what occurred on the playground.

Evaluation: The attached rubric can be utilized to assess the setting projects. Students should also submit their handouts of plot summaries based on the specific scenes at the end of the gallery walk. (*Note:* Some students are motivated by competition. If that is true of your class, students can also vote on the best-constructed setting model.)

BUILDING THE SETTING SAMPLE RUBRIC

The Giver **by Lois Lowry**
Building the Community Project

What? Create a visual model of Jonas's community in *The Giver.*

How? You may use any medium or type of materials to create your community.

Some examples are clay, poster board, a shoebox diorama, wood, Lego or other building blocks, or a video tour.

Directions:

1. *At least three* examples of structures or community details that are described in the book must be included.

2. These structures must be labeled.

3. Each label must include a passage from the text that supports and proves your vision of the structure.

For example: If you include a road with bicycles, you must find a passage from the text that explains that bicycles are the only mode of transportation in the village.

If you choose to work in groups, please be prepared to evaluate your partner's performance on the project.

> You will present your communities! Your classmates must be able to identify the scene or setting that you have re-created! Be prepared and consult the rubric!

The Giver by Lois Lowry: Community Model

Students' Names: _____

Category	A	B	C	D
Text-Based Structures	At least three accurate, text-based facts are displayed on the poster.	Two accurate facts are displayed on the poster.	One accurate fact is displayed on the poster.	No facts are included in the model.
Labels	All three structures are clearly labeled and passages are cited correctly.	All three structures are clearly labeled, but all passages are not cited correctly.	All three structures are labeled, but passages are not cited correctly.	No labels or correct citations.
Attractiveness	The model is exceptionally attractive in terms of design, layout, and neatness.	The model is attractive in terms of design, layout and neatness.	The model is acceptably attractive though it may be a bit messy.	The model is distractingly messy or very poorly designed. It is not attractive.
Creativity and Originality	Several of the graphics used on the project reflect an exceptional degree of student creativity in their creation and/or display.	One or two of the graphics used on the project reflect student creativity in their creation and/or display.	The graphics are made by the student, but are based on the designs or ideas of others.	No graphics made by the student are included.

Overall Grade: _____

Comments:

Lesson 26
DRAMA DIALOGUES

Level: For all levels (alternate modality: language arts)

Purpose: Many students are always more interested in a subject when they can get actively involved in a lesson and when they are responsible for the direction of the lesson. This strategy can be utilized in conjunction with all types of literature studies and genres, and is effective because it requires students to read text closely and then extract relevant selections and details.

Time: 60 minutes

Materials: Copies of selected text for each student; paper; pencil

Procedure: To create the dialogues, students first read a passage of text. After reading, the students are then challenged to remove and rearrange a selected number of lines of dialogue. These lines may be direct quotations as they appear in the text, or students may reorder character statements to create a unique conversation. The final dialogue exchange should accurately summarize one main aspect of the text. This strategy is most effective when students are paired together or placed in small groups, so that the lines can be reenacted after the dialogue scripts are created.

1. Provide a selection of text for students to read. The text should contain conversation between at least two characters; the number of characters in the text that are engaging in the conversation will dictate the size of student groups. (*Note:* Use a play to scaffold this strategy for students, as the character lines are already separated.)

2. After students have read the text silently, instruct them to summarize the main idea of the conversation and write it in paragraph form at the top of their paper. This paragraph summary can be omitted from the assignment as students become comfortable with the strategy; however, the paragraph is useful in guiding students as they extract dialogue lines.

3. The next step requires students to extract lines of character dialogue from the text and reorganize them into a new conversation that portrays the main idea of the text. Students should not recopy every single line of character conversation. Instead, they must carefully select and reorder the lines so that their dialogues accurately reflect the main ideas of the passage. You can provide the text in large print and have the students physically cut and paste the words on to another sheet, or you can have the students use the cut-and-paste function on a computer to reorder the lines.

4. Students then perform a dramatic reading of the conversation in front of classmates.

Evaluation: Since each group of students presents a different section of the text, the rest of the students should critique the presentation on the basis of how easy it is to determine what is going on in the scene. For each presentation, all of the other students will state who the characters are in the scene, what is going on in the scene, and where this scene fits into the whole story.

DRAMA DIALOGUE EXAMPLE FOR *JOHNNY TREMAIN*

If you are familiar with the story of Johnny Tremain, you will know that these words never actually appear in the book *Johnny Tremain* by Esther Forbes, but they might have.

Speaker 1: You, boy, come here.

Speaker 2: Me, sir? (looking around, but no one else is there)

Speaker 1: Yes, you. I need someone who can deliver these newspapers to the people outside of Boston who want to know what is going on. Can you ride?

Speaker 2: Ride a horse?

Speaker 1: Yes, a horse. Some of the people who want to read these live at quite a distance. Are you sure that your hand won't prevent you from handling a horse?

Speaker 2: Yes, sir, I can ride a horse.

Speaker 1: Good, then come back in three days and I'll tell you where and to whom to deliver these. This will be a dangerous job because the Redcoats may stop you, so you will need to be careful and cunning to avoid them.

Speaker 2: Who will be interested in a boy on a horse? I might have been running an errand in Boston and just coming back home or I might be looking for the doctor for a friend . . .

Speaker 1: Don't say anything about doctors. You may cause the Redcoats to think about Dr. Warren, and we don't want to get him into trouble.

Speaker 2: Yes, sir, I get the point. I'm to get the newspapers and take them to people you will tell me about who want to read them.

Lesson 27

INDEPENDENT READING RACE

Level: For all levels (incentive: language arts)

Purpose: This strategy involves creating a classroom competition for independent reading with the goal of increasing how much each student reads for enjoyment.

Time: At least 60 minutes of independent reading each week for 9 weeks

Materials:

- A large variety of independent texts, including contemporary novels, magazines, graphic novels, informational texts, dramas, and similar materials
- A class set of reading logs (folders or composition books)
- Materials for the independent book talk projects

Procedure: Students are allocated at least 60 minutes of independent reading each week, which can be organized in four 15-minute segments, two 30-minute segments, or one 60-minute segment. This time should be scaffolded for students, as many of them will not be able to read independently for 60 minutes at the beginning of the year. Also, various sharing activities should be incorporated into the sustained reading to help students remain focused and on-task (for example, after reading for 20 minutes, allow students to turn to a partner and explain their favorite passage from the reading). As students complete an independent text, they record the title, author, and a brief plot synopsis in their independent reading log. The novel's title and number of pages read are also recorded on a class log sheet. At the end of the quarter, students are responsible for creating a book talk project for at least one of their completed independent texts. This project could be visual, dramatic, oral, written, or video based. In addition, the total number of independent pages read is recorded on the class log sheet and totaled. The winning class (or group, if you split one class into different independent reading teams) is rewarded for being the winning reading team for the quarter. This award should be of significant value, as it works to motivate students for the remaining quarters. The student who read the most pages independently can also be rewarded, to motivate the high level readers.

1. Students are given at least 60 minutes of independent reading time each week, and students are given personal choice about the texts that they read. Some students may need to be matched with "just-right" books.

2. After students complete a text, they record the title, author, and number of pages in their reading logs. Students should also record the title and number of pages read on the class log.

3. While students read independently, the teacher should circulate throughout the room, privately asking questions and engaging in conversations about texts; modeling good independent reading habits by reading independently with the class; and collecting performance data, such as miscue analysis records or anecdotal records of fluency habits.

4. At the end of the quarter, students prepare a book review project for at least one of the books completed. A generic rubric can be used for all projects that includes categories for organization, story elements, and preparedness. The types of projects may include dioramas, oral book reports, monologues, talk shows, PowerPoint presentations, web pages, blogs, and the like. The point of the project is to review the text for the class.

Evaluation: The number of pages read by the entire class is totaled, and the winning class or team receives an award. The page number competition starts over at the start of the new quarter. This competition could also be tallied on a weekly basis, if students need additional motivation.

Lesson 28
ROUND-THE-ROOM PHOTO ALBUMS (pre- or postreading activity)

Level: For all levels (incentive or review: language arts, history, social studies, science)

Purpose: This strategy can be utilized as a prereading anticipation activity or as a postreading reflection activity. It is most efficient when used with a critical literacy text—that is, a text that discusses some type of controversial or complex social issue or injustice such as racism, the Holocaust, Japanese-American internment camps, or similar subjects.

This strategy involves the creation of multiple stations throughout the classroom; each station portrays a picture of a different aspect, theme, or main idea that is represented within the selected text. As students rotate throughout the classroom individually, they reflect and respond to each of the photographs; these reflections may be in the form of another picture, a poem, a word, sentence, or a paragraph.

Time: 45 minutes

Materials: Various picture stations set up in classroom; clipboards; response sheets; pencils

Procedure:

1. Provide a series of photographs that represent themes or main ideas within the text to be studied, and hang each picture in a different location in the classroom.

2. Instruct students to begin at the station closest to their individual desk and then travel to each station within the classroom. As they view each photograph, challenge students to reflect and respond with words or pictures. Their reflections should depict their feelings, questions, thoughts, and fears about the picture. The reflective writing is not for technical assessment, but rather for content and effort assessment only. Allow students a designated length of time at each station. This time should be monitored with a classroom timer or stop watch.

3. If this is used as a prereading activity: After students have viewed and responded to each picture, instruct them to make a prediction about the text that will be read. If it is used as a postreading activity: Based upon the photographs that were viewed, students should attempt to answer the 5 W's—*who, what, where, when,* and *why*—from the text.

4. Allow students to share reflections and predictions with their classmates.

Evaluation: This activity is designed to help students develop the ability to analyze and respond to different forms of information and to learn to express their responses to the sources. Success will be assessed on an individual basis.

EXAMPLES OF PICTURES FOR *JOHNNY TREMAIN*

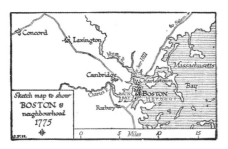

Lesson 29

PICTURE BOXES or COMIC STRIPS

Level: For all levels (alternative modality: any language-based material)

Purpose: Students are provided with various selections of text (for example, chapters from novels, picture books, and nonfiction articles); after independently reading the texts, students then respond with a reflective drawing on a provided handout. The students' drawings should depict the main idea of the textual selection or any part of the text that the student made connections with (either text-to-self, text-to-text, or text-to-world connections). After students draw reflections for each selection of text, they are then encouraged to share at least one drawing with the class. The final product resembles a comic strip.

Time: 60 minutes

Materials: Various selections of text about one theme; construction paper; colored pencils; rulers; markers

Procedure:

1. Choose a variety of texts that all center on one specific theme or concept. To complete this strategy in one class period, the average text length should be two pages or less. Students should spend 15 minutes or less with each text, including both reading and responding.

2. Instruct students to read a selection of text; this reading can be done individually or with a partner.

3. After students have read the text, challenge them to create a picture box that depicts the meaning. What elements or ideas were relevant or important within the text? What connections were made? The picture boxes should represent the student's interpretations of the meaning and importance of the text.

4. Allow students to share picture boxes with a partner or with the class.

Evaluation: Post the picture boxes. Each student will examine all of the pictures and decide what the common theme is for the texts. Then each student will write a sentence about how the pictures depict the theme.

Lesson 30
READ-ALOUD

Level: For all levels (incentive and enrichment: for all language-based material)

Purpose: This strategy involves creating a classroom competition for independent reading, with the goal of increasing how much each student reads for enjoyment

Time: 10 minutes (Read-Aloud should be incorporated as often as possible)

Materials: A large variety of Read-Aloud materials. Some examples include newspaper articles, comic strips, picture books, nonfiction articles, advertisements, obituaries, jokes, short stories, letters, and novel chapters.

Procedure:

According to Janet Allen in her text *Yellow Brick Roads: Shared and Guided Paths to Independent Reading*, "The single most important activity for building the knowledge required for eventual success is reading aloud to children" (p. 45). Students at all ages and stages of development make academic gains from being engaged in read-aloud experiences because they are able to identify and hear the qualities of good reading. Fluency, phrasing, voice intonation, self-monitoring, and questioning strategies are modeled for students as they actively participate in read-aloud experiences; furthermore, teachers can use reading aloud as a strategy to introduce and expose students to various types of books that may be above the appropriate skill level for shared or independent texts.

Read-Aloud should be incorporated into classroom procedures and activities on a routine basis and can be utilized to interest students in a specific topic, genre, or novel series, or to supplement content. Read-Aloud is a critical element to any literacy program because it provides students with an opportunity to *enjoy* literature. Students who claim that reading is an arduous school-related task are afforded the opportunity to enjoy and experience a story through Read-Aloud; and "for students who have had difficulty reading, [Read-Aloud] can be one of the times when language and literacy can be enjoyed with no risk" (Allen, 2000, p. 45).

1. Select a passage of text. The selected text can be based upon the daily lesson—some examples include reading aloud a comic strip on a day that students examine dialogue, reading aloud a picture book about World War II while students read the memoir of a Holocaust victim, reading aloud a Dr. Seuss picture book on a day that students examine author's craft and rhyme, or reading aloud a descriptive nonfiction article on a day that students examine adjective usage.

   The selected text can also be used to interest students in a particular genre, topic, or novel series. For example, the reading aloud of the first book in a high-interest young adult series will intrigue and interest students in the remaining texts in the series. We read the first book in the *On the Run* series by Gordon Korman to four groups of seventh and eighth grade boys, and they were so interested in the remaining story that many of them continued on to read the entire series.

2. While reading aloud to students, remember to be active and engaging. The delivery of the story is a key component in maintaining student interest. As teachers, we should not be reading aloud to our students in the same manner that news anchors deliver the stock reports. Instead, we must ensure that students are interested and engaged throughout the entire Read-Aloud.

3. To guarantee that students are actively engaged in the story, verbalize and model the actions that occur in a reader's mind by pausing to question characters' motives or predict upcoming events. But remember to question and observe as an equal participant in the reading—not as the all-knowing teacher. Students gain an understanding of active reading and listening as they watch you model and verbalize the behaviors of a fluent reader.

Also, engage students in different activities throughout the Read-Aloud in order to ensure participation and focus. For example, students may record their favorite passages from the Read-Aloud and share at the end, sketch their interpretations of the scene as it occurs, or write a haiku that addresses the main action of the chapter or scene. Remember, the active learner may be able to pay closer attention if his hands are busy.

Evaluation: At the completion of the Read-Aloud, encourage students to make connections with the reading. These connections can be text-to-text connections, text-to-self connections, or text-to-world connections. These class connections can be recorded on a wall chart and revisited at the completion of each daily Read-Aloud.

Lesson 31
READING BINGO

Level: Three levels supplied (incentive activity: for language arts)

Purpose: Getting active learners to read for pleasure can be difficult. Reading seems such a passive activity, and they can quickly become restless and bored. Approaches which recruit other interests will increase the possibility that the student will pick up a book. The idea here is that the charts give the students a tangible method to mark their progress and, if the students are competitive, help them engage in indirect competition—this is competition with one's self, attaining a personal best.

Time: Once you have introduced your class to the notion of Reading Bingo, which shouldn't take more than a few minutes, you may want to remind students once a week about maintaining their cards. Several times a year, you may schedule some time to reward students who have completed rows or entire cards.

Materials:

- Bingo cards. Samples are included here, but you can develop your own which will be responsive to the needs of your class. You can keep the cards in a ring-bound notebook, or each child can keep a card in her class portfolio. Because these cards will be around for a while, you may want to duplicate them on to stiff paper or card stock. You can laminate paper versions, but keeping the marks on the slick surface is difficult.
- Rewards which will reflect the age and interests of your students. Elementary students may be quite content with collecting stickers or stars, while older students may be more interested in winning a certificate for a personal pizza from a local restaurant.

Procedure:

1. Show the students the bingo cards you have selected. For differentiated classrooms, you can develop several different cards aimed at the different reading levels or interests of your students.

2. You can give students a bingo card, or you may choose to allow them to select one for themselves. Point out that to win a reward, they will need to complete a row across, down or diagonally. If you like, you can offer an additional reward to students completing an entire card.

3. Students should show you the book they have selected to read so that you can make a note of it. When they have completed the book, you may have younger children tell you their favorite scene or older students write a paragraph on their favorite character. When students complete a selection, they should bring the card to you to be marked.

4. Remind students periodically that they should be reading. It is important that children understand that they are to read books at their level and not at someone else's level.

5. You can display the completed cards or you can make a note of this in the child's file.

6. These should not be graded. The point is to encourage students to read for pleasure, not because they have to. If a student has poor participation in the program, you can encourage them by helping them select reading material that they find interesting, but they should not feel that they must read books that are not required for class. What you don't want to happen is for a student to feel as if reading is a burden or that the activity provides more evidence that he is an inadequate student.

Evaluation: Remember, these are not to be graded but serve as a method to help students acquire reading fluency. Yes, you want all students to participate, but students with poor reading skills may feel this is not for them. You may want to simplify the task for them—using chapters of a book in a square instead of an entire book or magazine in a square.

Other suggested categories not used on the attached cards might be:

- Magazine article
- Myth or legend
- Book with girl as main character
- Book with boy as main character
- How-to book or article
- Ancient culture book
- Teacher recommendation
- Place in the world book
- Peer recommendation
- Informational book
- Animal book

Name: _____

Rules: You can earn four bingos—horizontally or vertically! Each book only counts for one square. Have *fun*!

Autobiography	Folktale	Historical Fiction	Nonfiction
Realistic Fiction	Science	Fantasy	Biography
Poetry	Free Choice–Chapter Book	Mystery	Realistic Fiction
Science Fiction	Fantasy	Series	Easy Reader

7th Grade Reading BINGO

Name: _____

Rules: You can earn four bingos—horizontally or vertically! Each book only counts for one square.

Autobiography	Folktale	Historical Fiction	Nonfiction
Graphic Novel	Science	Fantasy	Biography
Poetry	Free Choice–Chapter Book	Mystery	Realistic Fiction
Science Fiction	Adventure	Series	Newspaper

10th Grade Reading Bingo

Name: _____

Rules: You can earn four bingos—horizontally or vertically! Each book only counts for one square.

Autobiography	Play	Historical Fiction	Nonfiction
Realistic Fiction	Research	Political or Psychological Thriller	Biography
Poetry	Literary or Historical Criticism	Classic Mystery	Folklore
Science Fiction	Essays	Series	Collection of Short Stories

Lesson 32

TEXT TABLEAUX

Level: For all levels, but best with younger grades (alternative modality: language arts)

Purpose: This strategy requires students to impersonate a character from a story and to reenact a specific scene from the text. After students have read a text, they are divided into partner groups. Each group then selects a scene from the text to act out for the class. After selecting a scene, students determine a way to "freeze" the scene. After the scene is frozen, one character "comes alive" and explains what he thinks is happening to the class. After the first character refreezes, the second character comes alive and gives her explanation for the events. Students in the class are encouraged to predict which scene will be reenacted based upon the frozen scene in the beginning of the text tableau.

Time: Two 60-minute periods

Materials: A text that the students have read; materials for possible costumes and props

Procedure:

1. On the first day, students are divided into partner groups and given a selection of text that they have already read.

2. Students choose a scene from the text to reenact.

3. Students create two paragraphs of dialogue that reflect the specific character's thoughts, opinions, emotions, intentions, etc. This dialogue should be a mix of actual text dialogue and invented dialogue based upon the students' interpretations of the characters (that is, what the students think the characters would say).

4. Students then decide on a pose to freeze that depicts the action of the scene.

5. Students prepare by memorizing lines and perfecting the frozen pose.

6. On the second day, each student group performs the text tableau presentation for the class. The performing group first freezes their scene. While the scene is frozen, the class is given the opportunity to write down predictions about which scene will be reenacted. After the class has finished predicting, the first actor "comes alive" and recites his two paragraphs of dialogue; the actor then refreezes and the second actor does the same. When both actors are finished speaking, the class is permitted to ask the "characters" questions about the scene (for example, "Why did you act that way?" and "How do you feel about another character?"). The student actors must remain in character to answer the questions.

7. This can be an extension of Drama Dialogues, Lesson 26. After the students present their dialogue, they then freeze and each character gives an interpretation of what is going on inside the character.

Evaluation: Two different sets of skills are at play in this activity. The first is that the actors must correctly portray the characters in their scene. How easy is it for the other students to determine the identity of each character? Do the other students believe the dialogue, and does what the students created seem true to the story? The second set of skills involves how well the observers can critically appraise the depictions. Can they identify actions and dialogue from the original story?

LANGUAGE ARTS LESSONS: Reading

Lesson 33
WRITING PROMPTS FOR ACTIVE LEARNERS

Level: For all levels (incentive activity: for all language-based material)

Purpose: Many writing prompts for students are not interesting to active learners. Try one of these!

Scary or thrilling

a. There I was, hanging by one hand from a windowsill on the top of the tallest building in town.

b. It wasn't the dark that bothered me, but the menacing growls that seemed to be all too close on the left.

c. Describe what goes through your mind second by second when you are on your favorite roller coaster.

d. Find out about spelunking and describe why it might be both scary and exciting to do that.

Sports

a. It was the most amazing catch I ever saw. Who knew he could do that?

b. Every sports story seems to end with the hero making the big play that saves the day. This story isn't like that at all.

c. Losing is not always the worst outcome; sometime winning is.

d. Going to live in a new country is hard enough without having to learn to play a sport you have never even heard of before.

Reality (even if they are made-up stories)

a. My grandfather (or appropriate family member) had the most remarkable experiences when he was young.

b. Our town is named for a man no one ever heard of, but his life was rather interesting.

c. Interview an adult. Describe their background and why they are involved in their present occupation.

d. Find out about your grandparents and great-grandparents, what their names were, where they were from, what they did, and how you and your family came to live where you do now.

Fantasy

a. I was simply walking down the street, and when I turned the corner I realized that I was now in a time 100 years earlier.

b. The thing, for it was hard to call it an animal, slid through the window before anyone could stop it.

c. My next door neighbor is a spy—that is the only explanation for his behavior.

d. Over the past several months, I have realized that I can understand what my dog is saying to me, not just in general terms, but specifically.

Humor

a. The autobiography of Humpty Dumpty. The King's men were out to get me!

b. What would happen if you were principal for a day?

c. Why my life should be a comedy show on TV.

d. Write down the funniest knock-knock joke you know and explain why it is funny.

Lesson 34
SIX DEGREES OF SEPARATION

Level: Suggestions provided for various levels (alternative modality and enrichment)

Purpose: Some children, particularly active learners, have trouble proofreading. This lesson gives them practice in seeing differences and similarities in words. The differences and similarities can first center on spelling and then as the students get better at the skill, the differences can be in meaning.

Time: Variable. This is best used as a homework assignment or an in-class filler for students who finish ahead of the rest of the class.

Materials: You will need to have examples to show the students what they are to do. When students are first learning the skill, select words which you know are fairly easy to work with.

Procedure: The procedure is to pick any two words and try to figure out how to get from one to the other either in meaning or spelling in six steps or less.

1. Show students examples of the procedure.

2. Changes in letters:

   a. Change in letters, but order stays the same:

      i. How do you get from *cat* to *bed* in six steps? *cat—hat—had—lad—led—bed*

      ii. How do you get from *need* to *loaf* in six steps? *need—reed—read—road—load—loaf*

      iii. How do you get from *clad* to *chat* in six steps (blends and digraphs may be treated as one letter)? *clad—clan—than—that—what—chat*

   b. Change in letters, or order can change, but not both at the same time:

      i. How do you get from *ear* to *ape* in six steps? *ear—eat—ate—tea—pea—ape*

      ii. How do you get from *some* to *meet* in six steps? *some—same—seam—team—teem—meet*

      iii. How do you get from *leash* to *leech* in six steps (blends and digraphs may be treated as one letter)? *leash—least—beast—beach—beech—leech*

3. Changes in usage

   a. Change in words, but the meaning stays the same—the word to be changed is in italics:

      i. Can you find six different words that mean the same as *happy*? *Glad, cheery, joyful, on cloud nine, delighted, pleased*

      ii. Can you find six different ways to say: The boat *neared* the dock? The boat *approached* the dock; the boat *floated to* the dock; the boat *sailed to* the dock; the boat *almost touched* the dock; the boat *came close to* the dock; the boat *was next to* the dock.

    iii. Can you find six synonyms for *laughable* with at least two different meanings? *Risible, ludicrous, farcical, droll, pathetic, insulting*—some of the words mean *laugh with*, others mean *laugh at*.

b. Change in meaning, but the words stay the same:

    i. Use the word *run* in sentences with yourself, with pets, with rain, with food, with a car, and with a computer. *I run fast; My dog runs after the ball; The rain runs down the window; The syrup runs over the pancakes; The car engine runs now that my daddy fixed it;* and *The computer is running on Windows.*

    ii. Create sentences using the word *present* as an adjective, as a noun, and at least two sentences in which it has different meanings as a verb: *She was present in class; I got presents for my birthday; He presented the trophy to the winning team; Let me present my grandmother to you.*

    iii. Use the word *close* in six different ways: *I am close to you; close the door; the business closed down; She is my closest friend; He is close-minded; I am closing the floor to suggestions.*

Evaluation: While the object of the lesson is to get all of the parts correct, not all students will be able to do this well. This activity is designed to strengthen vocabulary and to give students practice in proofreading by picking up differences in words. Students can also develop their own patterns once they are familiar with the exercise.

Lesson 35
ABUNDANT ADJECTIVES and VERBS ALIVE!

Level: For all levels (enrichment and incentive: for language-based material)

Purpose: Some students do not develop extensive vocabularies and tend to use the same words over and over. This exercise is designed to help all students add words to their active vocabularies as well as to understand that synonyms may not convey exactly the same meaning—the difference between *connotation* and *denotation*. While the directions are designed for adjectives and verbs, you can easily develop similar exercises for other parts of speech.

Time: From 10 to 30 minutes, depending on how much you want the students to get from the exercise. Also suitable for homework.

Materials:

- List of vocabulary words, which can be developed from the material that is being read in class or from other sources.
- Students should have access to a dictionary, a thesaurus, a computer with a thesaurus, or other lists of synonyms and antonyms.

Procedure:

Part 1: Each student or pair of students selects one word from a list of vocabulary words. The students then use a dictionary, thesaurus, or any other source to develop a list of synonyms for the word they have selected. They then make up a simple sentence in which that word appears. Those lists and sentences are then handed in to the teacher.

Part 2: Display one of the sentences, and ask the class to come up with synonyms for the indicated word without using any sources. Use each synonym in the original sentence, discussing how the meaning of the sentence has changed from the original.

or

Part 2: Distribute the sentences to the students with the target word in each sentence underlined, italicized, or marked in some similar fashion. Students are then to come up with as many synonyms as they can for the marked words. Once students have their lists of words, display the sentence and ask the students to suggest replacement words. Discuss how the different replacements change the sense of the sentence.

Evaluation: Because each word has a different number of synonyms, students cannot be compared on the number of synonyms they find for their word. So, compare the number of synonyms that each student comes up with for the same word. If the students compiling the original list found more words, they get points, and students should receive points for every word suggested that was not included in the original list. A competition can be devised for the vocabulary king—the student who can come up with the greatest number of synonyms.

The second part of the lesson, determining the difference between the precise meaning of a word and its connotation, can be demonstrated by having the students use synonyms in the same sentence and discussing what the difference is in meaning.

ABUNDANT ADJECTIVES and VERBS ALIVE!
Worksheet Example

Adjectives

If the word is *big* and the sentence is *The big dog ran over to me*, synonyms would be *large, huge, enormous, gigantic, ginormous* (which has just been added to the dictionary), or *immense*. In a thesaurus, there may be other categories of synonyms for *big*, illustrating that the word is used to indicate more than just size. Other categories include some using *big* to describe a number of items, as in "The school is really big." That may mean that the building is large, but it may also mean that there are a lot of students who attend the school. Students need to indicate where the meaning of the sentence makes some synonyms inappropriate; for example, using *big* with *dog* probably does not indicate a large number of dogs but refers to the size of the dog.

Sample Worksheets

The _____ dog ran over to me

Synonyms	Connotation
big	dog is larger than average
large	pretty much the same as big
huge	bigger dog than a big one
enormous	not only very big, but also big around
gigantic	largest dog
ginormous	bigger dog than the person has ever seen
immense	biggest dog around as well as tall
important	leader of the pack

Verbs

If the word is *ran* and the sentence is *The big dog ran over to me*, synonyms for *run* (the present tense of *ran*) would include *sprint, move fast, race, rush,* or *flow.* Like *big, run* has a number of synonyms which involve ideas other than the speed at which one is moving; for example, *running a business* means to be in charge of the business and *running a machine* means to operate the machine.

The big dog _____ over to me

ran	faster than a walk
sprinted	faster than running
moved fast	same as ran
raced	fast with some competition involved
rushed	fast and hurried
flowed	smooth movement, not as fast as ran and probably not applied to dogs

Lesson 36
CONSTRUCTING LANGUAGE

Level: Two levels provided (lesson and alternative modality: all writing lessons)

Purpose: Getting active learners to look at word selection in a sentence and parts of speech can be difficult. It can also be a challenge to get these students to understand what a topic sentence is, what a transition sentence looks like, and how a good paragraph is framed. This exercise provides an active way to examine how to build a sentence and how to build a paragraph.

Time: From 10 to 45 minutes, depending on the level of your students and how much you want the students to get from the exercise

Materials: Sentences or paragraphs which have been printed out, then cut apart and put into small zipped plastic bags according to the procedure below

Procedure:

Making the sentence bags

(*Warning:* Try not to use sentences with one-letter words such as *a* or *I*. Those are easy to lose.)

For younger students, select two sentences from a text they are reading and print them out with appropriate capitalization, punctuation, and other grammatical notation. Enlarge the sentences using a font size of 36 or 48 points and print on card stock. Cut the words apart and put them in a bag.

For older students, select two sentences and print them out without any capitalization, punctuation, or other notation. Enlarge, print on card stock, and cut apart.

Making the paragraph bags

For students at all levels, print on card stock two consecutive paragraphs from something they have been reading. Retype the sentences so that each starts at the beginning of the line; otherwise, the students can get the correct configuration simply by fitting the shapes together. Enlarge slightly; 18-point type is better than 12-point type.

Have the students form groups of two and give each group one of the bags with the instruction to arrange the words into two sentences or to arrange the sentences into two paragraphs.

Students will ask if they have to use all of the words; the answer is *Yes*.

Give the students enough time to work with the materials for a bit and then ask questions such as:

For word bags:

1. What meaning, story, or event do you think the sentences are trying to convey?

2. Are there any groups of words which seem to belong together?

3. As you drift around the room, look to see if students are using the same word in different ways. If so, write that word on the board and ask questions such as "What do you think the meaning of this word is?" "Is every group using it as the same part of speech?"

4. If you don't have the same word order as the original, do your sentences convey the same meaning?

5. Does it make a difference to the meaning of the sentences to move certain words around?

6. Can you use these words to make sentences with entirely different meaning?

For sentence bags:

1. What are the two topic sentences for each set of paragraphs? What makes them topic sentences?

2. How did you decide to put the sentences in paragraphs?

3. Are there any transition sentences?

4. What is the purpose of the other sentences?

5. Does it make a difference to the meaning of the paragraph if the sentences are in a different order?

6. Are there any sentences which are unnecessary (that could be removed without changing the sense of the paragraph)? If so, why is that sentence in there?

Evaluation: The only evaluation will be your observations of student engagement and understanding. This exercise is best used to solidify information learned in class. You can give students sample sets for homework, which will allow them to take more time to come up with solutions.

CONSTRUCTING LANGUAGE SAMPLE SENTENCES AND PARAGRAPHS

Sentences for younger students:

His favorite season of the year was summer. He visited his grandparents, played ball with his friends, and just did nothing.

Paragraphs for younger students:

When Harry came out of his house, he realized that it had stormed last night.

He could see the puddles of water and the sticks and leaves that had fallen from the big tree in the yard.

When his father saw what was all over the lawn, he made Harry pick up everything that had fallen on the grass.

The tree shaded the front of the house, but sometimes he wished it wasn't there.

- -

In the meantime, Harry decided he would play in the big puddle at the end of the driveway.

He got a few small sticks and made a little raft using a big leaf for a sail.

Before he had a chance to find out if it would float, his father was on the front porch calling him to clear the lawn of what had fallen during the storm.

Sentences for older students:

when sam heard the savage war whoop of his enemies behind him he glanced quickly back over the tail of his buckskin pony what he saw made his heart pound against his ribs

Paragraphs for older students:

Pick something from what you are reading. This excerpt is from *Abe Lincoln Grows Up* (Sandburg, 1953, p. 67).

The whole family pitched in and build a pole-shed or "half-faced camp."

On a slope of ground stood two trees about fourteen feet apart, east and west.

These formed the two strong corner posts of a sort of cabin with three sides, the fourth side open, facing south.

The sides and the roof were covered with poles, branches, brush, dried grass, mud; chinks were stuffed where the wind or the rain was trying to come through.

At the open side a log fire was kept burning night and day.

In the two far corners inside the camp were beds of dry leaves on the ground.

To these beds the sleepers brought their blankets and bearskins.

- -

Here they lived a year.

In summertime and in fair weather, the pole-shed was snug enough.

When the rainstorms or wind and snow broke through and drenched the place, or when the south or southwest wind blew the fire smoke into the camp so those inside had to clear out, it was a rough life.

Lesson 37

GRAMMAR RUMMY or GO FISH FOR GRAMMAR

Level: Two levels provided (alternative modality and enrichment: for grammar lesson)

Purpose: While grammar has rules that make it an easier subject for active learners, it is sometimes hard for those learners to get the fine points, such as agreement between subject and verb or placement of words in a sentence for emphasis. This game is designed to help students appreciate the order of words in a sentence.

Time: At least 20 minutes to play one round. Time will vary depending on how much you want the students to get from the exercise.

Materials: Make a set of cards which can be used over and over for this game. Start with colored 3-by-5-inch index cards cut in half widthwise so that the sections are now 3 by 2.5 inches. Assign a color to each part of speech, such as red for verbs, yellow for nouns, green for adjectives, white for articles, and so forth. Have your students copy one word on to each card of the appropriate color.

Procedure: To play Go Fish for Grammar for younger students: Deal five cards to each student and pile the remaining cards face down in the middle of the table. Since the color of the cards tells other students what parts of speech a student has, the rules have to be a bit more specific. Instead of asking for a noun, a student has to be specific and ask another student for a noun that is a place or a verb that means an action. If the student being asked doesn't have such a card, that student tells the one who asked "Go fish," and the asker takes a card from the pile in the middle. As a student develops sentences, she can put the cards down in the proper order when it is her turn. The student who goes out first wins.

To play Rummy for older students: Shuffle the cards—it is difficult to shuffle these cards as you would with playing cards, so just put all the cards face down on a table and move them around. Each student will hold the cards as with regular playing cards, so that others cannot see the words. To begin the game, each student will be dealt five words (for younger students) or seven words (for older students); as their skills improve, the number of words can be increased up to ten. Stack the rest of the cards in the middle, still face down. Each student gets a turn to draw one card from the top of the deck and discard a card face up. Students may pick the last discarded card instead of the top card of the deck and then discard a card they already hold. Students may also elect to skip a turn if the words available don't help them (which they can tell from the color of the card), but they don't get two turns in a row later. When a student can make a sentence with his words, he puts them down at once and gets as many points as he has words in his sentence. He gets the points only when he can make all the words agree correctly and he has them in the correct order to make sense. For example, on the cards, verbs will be in the infinitive form. Students must then say how the verb will change to fit the sentence he is making. The rest of the players put their cards down and can get points for as much of their hand as will make a sentence, losing points for useless words. If you are not sure of the rules of rummy, check for rules for playing rummy on the Internet or in a book of card games.

For younger students, provide plain white cards with conjunctions and articles on them, and allow the students to use as many as they need to create a sentence with the words in their hand. For older students, include those cards in the deck as part of the regular play.

Evaluation: Students can keep track of the points accumulated, which can be kept as a running total or can just be used to determine the winner for the day. The teacher should keep track of each winning sentence. As students become more expert at this game, they will need to increase the number of words used. You can have an advanced game which requires either a compound sentence or some sort of clause.

Lesson 38
HEADLINES, EPITAPHS, AND TWEETS

Level: For all levels (lesson and enrichment: for language arts)

Purpose: One of the problems that some active learners have in learning to write is that they find it difficult to produce a great many words. While other students seem to have no trouble producing several pages on an assigned topic, these students may find it difficult to produce several paragraphs. The point of this exercise is to get all students thinking about a story, but only having to write a few words. The exercise on headlines and tweets is for all students, but the part on epitaphs is for older students.

Time: This lesson will take several days. You may want to repeat it several times in a school year. The introductory lesson on headlines and epitaphs should not take more than 30 minutes. Much of the writing will be done either as homework or in an assigned writing block.

Materials: Recent local newspapers; lists of epitaphs, which can be found on the Internet or in various literary sources. You can find epitaphs at: www.webpanda .com/ponder/epitaphs.htm, www.hauntedbay.com/thelab/epitaphs.shtml, and www.quotemountain.com/sayings/funny_tombstone_sayings.html. The epitaph lesson might be used around the time of Halloween, as many epitaphs appear on tombstones.

Procedure:

1. Begin the first lesson with a discussion of how headlines convey a great deal of information in a few words or how epitaphs try to characterize a person in a phrase or short poem.

2. Have students type headlines from newspapers onto a document and use the word count feature, which will also reveal how many characters are used. It is not the number of words but the space taken up that determines the length of a headline, and number and width of characters determines the space used.

3. Practice coming up with headlines for events that are happening in the students' lives, such as the outcome of a recent athletic contest or a new set of rules imposed by the administration. Practice coming up with epitaphs using cartoon characters or characters in their favorite video games.

4. Divide a story that the students have read into sections and assign each section to a pair of students. They are to come up with a headline for the major event in the assigned section or an epitaph for a character in that section.

5. Post the headlines or epitaphs around the classroom. Each student will go around the classroom, look at each headline or epitaph, and try to figure out the event or person they represent.

6. Twitter is a form of communication which limits the writer to 140 characters. While this is an informal form of writing, you can ask your students to describe an event in a book or an episode in history using the Twitter style. It is up to you whether or not *u wil acpt ltrs or nbrs 4 wrds*. However, if you have a hard time reading that phrase, you may want your students to complete what they are writing. By the way, the phrase in italics is only 23 characters; if written out completely (*you will accept letters or numbers for words*), the phrase is 44 characters.

Evaluation: Students will turn in their guesses. They win a point each time a student correctly guesses what their headline or epitaph refers to.

Lesson 39
PHONIC PHUN

Level: For all levels (enrichment and problem solving skills: for language arts)

Purpose: Some students either don't hear as well as the majority of students in your class or have not had much practice in listening to others. For whatever reason, you will find that some students have trouble with *phonemic awareness*, which is a key skill to learning reading. Helping all students learn to hear differences in sounds will help them with spelling, word recognition, and listening in class.

Time: From 5 to 20 minutes, depending on how much you want the students to get from the exercise

Materials: The complexity of words you select will depend on the level of your students. Begin by picking words from spelling or vocabulary lists, so that they are familiar with some of the words. For younger children, it will be enough simply to replace consonants or add or remove a trailing *e*. For older children, begin with simpler tasks and then make them more complicated, such as changing diphthongs, spelling homonyms, or any change in a word which connects spelling with sound.

Procedure: This is an example of how this strategy works. You simply start with one word and ask the students to change it. The number of changes you ask the students to make is only limited by your ability to think of changes. In the following examples, what you say is in bold and what the students write is italicized.

For younger students

Write the word **TOY** on your sheet: *TOY*

Now, change the **T** to a **B** and write that word on your sheet: *BOY*

Change the **O** to an **A** and write that word on your sheet: *BAY*

Change the **B** to a **D** and write that word on your sheet: *DAY*

Change the **Y** to a **D** and write that word: *DAD*

Change the **A** to a **U** and write that word: *DUD*

Add an **E** to the end of the word (this for slightly older students): *DUDE*

Then ask the students to read the words they have written. Point out how the sound of the words they have made changes as the letters change—*day* has a different sound for *a* than *dad* because of the effect of following letter, and the *u* in *dud* and *dude* has a very different sound because of the trailing *e*.

For older students

For older students, the lesson is the same, but you are using more complicated sounds—when you direct the students to make changes, give them the sound of the letter not the letter itself:

Write the word *SHELL* on your sheet: *SHELL*

Change the /sh/ sound to a /t/ sound and write that word: *TELL*

Change the /e/ sound to an /ie/ sound and write that word: *TILL*

Change the last *l* to an *e* and write that word (in this case actually say the names of the letters): *TILE*

Change the /t/ sound to a /wh/ sound and write that word: *WHILE*

Change the *ile* sound to an *ite* sound and write that word (you will not spell the sounds to be changed but sound them out): *WHITE*

Change the /wh/ to a /b/ and write that word: *BITE*

Drop the trailing *e* and write that word: *BIT*

Select students to read out the words they have written. Discuss how different sounds are made by different arrangement of letters: for example, how *i* is pronounced differently depending on whether the word ends in a double consonant or in a trailing *e*.

Evaluation: Evaluation will be student improvement in spelling and phonemic awareness. This exercise is best used to solidify information learned in class.

Lesson 40
POETRY CONSTRUCTION

Level: For all levels (incentive activity and enrichment: for language arts)

Purpose: Active learners will write poetry when there are specific rules to follow. The following five types of poems can be funny, weird, or exciting; but once they get the hang of making them, all students will enjoy writing these poems. Very young children can construct haiku once they are familiar with the patterns. Older elementary students are ready to write cinquains and diamantes, and children in middle school usually have the metacognition necessary to develop the pun or other form of humor in a limerick. Students in high school can certainly write all three, and their poems will reflect their vocabulary development and more sophisticated thinking ability. Poems for two voices do not require sophisticated vocabulary, but do require critical thinking.

Time: Introduction takes about 10 minutes; then give the students around 20 minutes to try to write a poem for themselves. These can be assigned for homework as well.

Materials: To start this exercise, you need to collect at least 10 samples of each type of poem and develop some method to display the poems together either on an interactive whiteboard, on an overhead projector, or on large Post-It sheets that can be hung from the walls of your classroom. There are many websites where you can find samples of these poetry styles; the librarian at your school will be happy to help you find books of poems for your students to enjoy.

Procedure: Each lesson should center on one type of poem only. Let the students become proficient with one type before you show the next one. You may not even want to present all types in the same school year. Help your students to understand that rhyme is not part of the first two types of poem. They are more about the pattern of the words and following the rules.

Do not tell the students what the names of the types of poetry are or what the rules are to begin with (this is crucial!). Put several examples of the same type on the board at the same time or display them on an interactive whiteboard or on a screen. Don't tell the students anything; first ask the students to find the common elements in the poems. Guide the students to discover the rules for each type. The rules for the first two and the fourth can be somewhat flexible, whereas the rules for the third type are a bit more rigid (although there is variability here as well). For younger students, make sure that all the poems displayed follow the same rules. Poems for older students may have more variable patterns.

The key to this exercise is that the teacher does not tell the students anything about the poems, but only asks questions to help the students find out how the poems are constructed. The point is that the experiential learner will remember the rules better if she figures them out for herself. She is less likely to remember when the teacher lectures.

Sample questions

What do the poems have in common? How are they different? Can you see any patterns in the way the poems are written? Is the shape of the poems similar? How about the rhythm? Can you find the similarity among the sample poems? Do any of the words rhyme? What about the topics of the poems? Are any alike? How about the number of syllables?

1. A *haiku* has three lines. Lines one and three have five syllables each, and line two has seven syllables. Here is an example:

   I am going home

   Even though you say to stay

   Home is where I go

2. A *cinquain* has five lines. Line one is one word, which is the title of the poem. Line two is two words that describe the title, line three is three words that tell action, line four is four words that express feeling, and line five is one word that reminds the reader of the title.

   Home

   My family

   Hugging, fighting, caring

   We stand as one

   Together

   In some versions, the last line is the same as the first line; in others the last line is one word that repeats the idea of the first line.

3. A *diamante* has seven lines and can be written by one student or by two. The first and seventh lines are single words that are contrasting. The second line is two adjectives that describe the first word, and the sixth line is two adjectives that describe the last word. The third line is three action verbs that describe or are connected to the first word, and the fifth line is three action verbs that go with the final word. The fourth line is four words, two going with the first word and two with the last. The writers can decide if the words alternate or follow each other. Students can be given the contrasting pair of words, write one part of the poem, and then meld the two halves, or they can write the poem together from the start.

   Summer

   Hot, green

   Swimming, running, playing

   Vacation, school, July, January

   Snowing, shivering, studying

   Cold, brown

   Winter

4. A *limerick* is a bit harder because the rules are very specific. Lines one, two, and five have the same number of syllables and rhyme with each other. The syllables can be as few as seven or as many as ten. Lines three and four rhyme with each other and have as few as five syllables or as many as seven. These lines should be shorter than lines one, two, and five. The final rhyme scheme is *aabba*. For students who have trouble finding words that rhyme, they can get help at www.rhymezone.com. In general, limericks are meant to be funny, with the last line offering a pun, a surprise, or some other twist on the story.

The woods was a place he would go

To think by himself in the snow

It got a bit icy

And walking was dicey

To get home he used a ski tow

If you say this poem out loud, it is easy to find the meter or rhythm in the poem, which is very specific for a limerick. A line can have the correct number of syllables but not be a good line for the poem as it does not follow the correct rhythm.

5. A *poem in two voices* is a poem written by two people; their two voices are represented by writing their parts in the left and right columns respectively on a page. The students can each start by describing themselves in a phrase; these two phrases together form the title of the poem. The next line is something they can say together which is true of both of them; it should be written twice, once on each side of the page. The poem continues going from the voices of the individuals to their joint voice. Lines written twice on the same line are said together; lines written alone on the left are read only by that individual and those on the right by that individual. Sometimes the lines designed to be said together are opposites of each other. Here's an example:

Humpty Dumpty and Tweedledum

Round as round can be	*Round as round can be*
Falling down	
	Agrees to have a battle
No one takes me seriously	*No one takes me seriously*
King's men	
	Queen's man

See the following worksheet for an example of how students can write this so that it is easier for them to read it as they get used to this form.

For more examples look for two books by Paul Fleischman, *I am Phoenix: Poems for Two Voices* (1985) and *Joyful Noise: Poems for Two Voices* (1988) both published by HarperCollins.

Evaluation: The mark of success is an original poem which fits the rules of a specific type of poem and conveys some message or idea. The poems given as examples here were written by one of the authors of this book and are not intended to be examples of great poetry. However, they follow the rules and would be acceptable illustrations of each type.

POEMS IN TWO VOICES Worksheet

Name: _____

Sample

Title	Humpty Dumpty	Tweedledum
Together	Round as round can be	Round as round can be
Humpty Dumpty	Falling down	
Tweedledum		Agrees to have a battle
Together	No one takes me seriously	No one takes me seriously
Opposites	King's men	
		Queen's man

The students decide on the theme, which should be two things that can be opposites. An example would be a circle and a square. Down the side, they decide which lines will be together and which different, and then in the squares under their part of the poem, they write in what they want to say.

Title		

Lesson 41
SONNET SETUP

Level: For older students (lesson: for language arts)

Purpose: One of the easiest poem forms for many students to deal with is the sonnet, because of the rules. This technique can be used with any passage in which you want the students to see the mechanics of poetry, as this will allow students to see how poems are shaped. Because of the complexity of the sonnet, this lesson is for older students.

Time: Around 30 to 45 minutes (with follow-up questions)

Materials: Select a number of sonnets as examples. Determine how you will display each sonnet and be able to mark it up so that the marks can be separated from the poem. A interactive whiteboard is the easiest to use. If you are able to project from your computer, display the poem on a whiteboard. If you do not have any projection equipment, copy the sonnet on to an acetate sheet for your overhead projector and use water-based markers on a separate covering sheet.

Procedure:

1. Select several sonnets and enter them into your computer or copy them on to sheets for the overhead projector. You can find a great many sonnets at www.sonnets.org.

2. Display the sonnet in the classroom. Invite a student to go to the board or come to the projector and underline the first words he sees that rhyme. Keep asking students to come forward until all rhymes are noted. You may not have enough colors to do this; if so, use a colored box around the words or circle the words.

3. Ask the students if they see any patterns. Actually, your students will probably see the pattern long before the last lines. Make sure that they note the couplet at the end. Point out that the rhyme in a Shakespearean sonnet scheme is *abab cdcd efef gg*. A Spenserian sonnet scheme is *abab bcbc cdcd ee*. An Italian sonnet scheme is *abba abba cde cde*.

4. Then have a student highlight or draw a box around all the lines with the *abab* rhyme scheme. Follow that by asking students to highlight separately the *cdcd* and *efef* lines. How many lines are those? Ask them what these words have in common: *quarter, quart, quadruplets, quadrant, quadruped*. All refer to something made of four parts, so four lines of poetry grouped together are called a *quatrain*.

5. Point to the two lines at the end. Ask them: If a group of four people is a *quartet*, what is a group of two people? A *couple*, so the two lines at the end are a *couplet*.

6. Ask the students to note where the periods come in the lines in the sonnet. Do they follow the same scheme as the rhyme does? (Sometimes they will and sometimes they won't.) How about the ideas in the poem? Are they divided by quatrains?

7. When you have completed looking at the shape of the first sonnet, put a second sonnet up without removing the colored markings. While the placement of the rhyming words will not be exactly the same, ask the students to look at the new sonnet and see if the rhyme scheme is the same as the first sonnet. Ask the same questions about the new poem that you asked about the original poem.

8. Divide the class into small groups. Instruct each group to come up with the rules for a sonnet. Give the students around 5 minutes to do this, and then have one person from each group come up and write the rules for sonnets that her group discovered. Compare the rules to develop a comprehensive description of sonnets.

9. Provide a different sonnet to each group of students. Give the groups 10 minutes or so to analyze the new poem according to rhyme, rhythm, and subject matter.

10. Have the students write a sonnet of their own.

Evaluation: The students will be able to develop a sonnet of their own. They can then share their sonnets with the class as well as provide an analysis of their poem according to this pattern.

Lesson 42
ROOTS AND STEMS

Level: For students fifth grade and above (problem solving and enrichment: for language arts)

Purpose: A strong vocabulary is built, not memorized. When students begin to recognize that parts of words have significance and that they can figure out the meaning of the word by knowing what the parts mean, they will become intrigued. Tell active learners that knowing this information is like understanding what the various parts of an engine do so that you can understand how the engine works when the parts are together.

Time: About 20 to 30 minutes to introduce the game. Once the students know the rules, the activity can be used whenever a suitable word comes up in class.

Materials:

- The Roots and Stems sheet
- A dedicated section in a notebook
- Dictionary

Procedure:

1. Put up a list of words, probably 10 or so, from recent reading. The words should be selected because they have prefixes or suffixes that modify the main part of the word. Some of the words should have either similar prefixes and suffixes or the same root word. Such words might include:

   a. *decline, incline*

   b. *submachine, submarine, substitute*

2. Have the students define the words

3. Explain that many words are made up of parts: the *root* of a word is the part that tells you what the word is about, and the *stems* are the prefixes and suffixes that are attached to the front or the back of the root and modify or shape the root.

4. Give the students the worksheet, which has one example worked for them. They will then use a dictionary to find the roots and stems of a number of words. Older students can note what is the source of the root, such as if the word is of Greek or Latin origin.

5. There are a number of ways to introduce this game. Students can be paired up and compete to find all the roots and stems of the same words, or students can draw words out of a hat.

6. Once students are familiar with finding roots and stems, you can give them words to analyze at home, or you can challenge students to find words with roots and stems in material in class.

7. For homework, students can keep lists of the roots and stems in a portion of their class notebook.

8. Older students can invent words using the roots and stems. Make sure that they understand that combining words from different origins such as a Greek root and a Latin stem does not usually produce a correct word.

Evaluation: Students will be able to use a dictionary with greater ease and will be able to figure out the meaning of many words without using a dictionary. Understanding roots and stems will also give students the origin and history of a word, which will increase the chance that they will learn to spell words better.

ROOTS AND STEMS Worksheet

Name: _____

Word	Root	Stem	Meaning
Polyglot	*glot* = tongue	*poly* = many	Having many tongues or speaking many languages

Lesson 43
LITERARY SCAVENGER HUNTS

Level: Can be adapted for all levels (review and incentive activity: for language-based courses)

Purpose: Proofreading is a very hard skill for many students to learn. Any activity which involves looking carefully at written material and allows students to compete will help them get better at this skill. There are several different versions of this idea, but they should all involve competition, either to finish first or to find the most of whatever they are looking for. While the students should work on these activities in pairs, individuals should keep a running total of their individual scores, because you will change the pairings so that students learn to work with everyone in the class.

Time: Anywhere from 10 minutes to several weeks, depending on how much you want the students to get from the exercise and what is involved

Materials: Once you have decided which type of hunt best fits your material, develop the list of items which will be used. Make sure that you give specific instructions, so that students are clear about what they are looking for as well as what will constitute a correct solution to the hunt. You should also be very clear about what sources students may use for the hunt. Will you allow them to use the Internet? May students ask others—parents, other teachers, older students—for assistance? Also, you may want to provide an example of how the results are displayed—do you want a narrative, or will a chart do? What you probably don't want is students bringing in the book with the locations of the information marked with slips of paper.

Procedure:

A. Easter egg hunt

Your students will tell you that an Easter egg is not necessarily a colored hen's egg, but a hidden feature on a DVD or software application that usually is something interesting or funny. In this hunt, students will be looking for something purposely hidden.

1. For young children, the objects do not have to be deeply hidden. They can look for all of the descriptions of the setting in a story they are reading or all of the words used to describe one of the characters.

2. Characters in books are frequently named something that either means something to the character or to the author. Find out the meaning hidden in the names of these characters: Templeton in *Charlotte's Web* by E. B. White, HAL in *2001: A Space Odyssey* by Arthur C. Clarke, Argus Filch in J. K. Rowling's *Harry Potter*, Saphira the dragon in *Eragon* by Christopher Paolini, and Cassie in Mildred D. Taylor's *The Road to Memphis* (story about the Logan family).

3. Many people have hidden to escape from bad events. For example, Anne Frank hid in an attic during World War II. Find four other people or groups of people, either historical figures or fictional characters, who hid. Describe who they were, why they hid, how they hid, and whether they were ever found.

B. Archeology treasure hunt

As the name implies, students must dig to find the treasure. They will be looking for something in the background or the history of the material.

1. Using a map of your local area or a list of names of nearby streets and towns, the students can search to find out where the names came from. For example: where did the name *New York* come from, and did the city have earlier names?

2. What are five facts about the life of Harper Lee that the author has in common with Scout, the major character in *To Kill a Mockingbird*? Give your sources for the facts about Harper Lee and the page number for the facts about Scout.

3. Works of *historical* fiction are based on real events but use fictional characters to tell the story. The book *Echoes of Andersonville* by Robert Diel Dean is about the most famous prison camp during the Civil War. After reading the book, look up facts about the Andersonville prison on the Internet. Find five facts in the book that actually happened during the war and find five that the author made up.

C. Pirate treasure hunt

In this version, a map must be followed or made to find the treasure. You can provide the map or require the students to construct the map.

1. Using the *Undersea Encounters* series by Mary Jo Rhodes and David Hall, students can find the locations where the animals described in the books can be found. Using the *True Books: American History Series,* published by the Children's Press, students can locate where the events took place.

2. The story *Johnny Tremain*, by Esther Forbes, takes place in Boston just before the start of the Revolutionary war. Using a map of pre-Revolutionary Boston, place on it the location of the major events in the book. Make sure you make specific reference to the page numbers in your book for each event.

3. *Dove* by Robin L. Graham is the story of a boy who at 16 years old began to sail around the world and finished his trip 4 years later. Using a map of the world, find all the places mentioned in the book where Graham lands, giving the approximate date. On the same map, follow the path of Captain James Cook's first trip around the world in a sailing vessel in the 18th century. See if Graham and Cook landed in any of the same places or had similar experiences.

D. I spy

A more sophisticated version of the old game. You define the categories, and the students have to find exemplars of each category.

1. In the story we are reading, find five animals that are mentioned; or five colors; or five nouns and five verbs.

2. In the story we are reading, find five instances of subject-verb agreement with an intervening phrase or clause; five instances of verbs used in the past tense; five instances of pronoun agreement (indicating the pronoun and the noun to which the pronoun refers); five metaphors and five similes.

3. In the story we are reading, find three different descriptions of the physical aspects of one person in the story and three different descriptions of the character of that same person. Find another person in the story who is very different from the person you have chosen and find three physical descriptions and three character descriptions. Compare the descriptions to show how those individuals are different from each other.

Evaluation: All of these hunts involve some form of competition, but not at the price of careless work. Finishing first should not be the sole basis for awarding points; you should have a structure for points so that students win points for being first to complete the hunt, but also for using the most sources, for finding the most varied items, for spelling everything correctly (but not for neatness), or for whatever fits the type of hunt you have selected.

Lesson 44

SUPERBOWL WRITERS

Level: Intended for middle school students, but can be adapted (incentive activity: for language) arts

Purpose: Many active learners have trouble getting excited about writing. This will provide a writing prompt that will excite them and about which they will want to write.

Time: 30 minutes for the video; several 20-minute sections for the writing and revision portion

Materials: The coaching staff at your school may be able to supply you with a video of one exciting play during a football game, or you may find a DVD with clips from sports games. Any sport can be used, but the nature of football means that it is easier to start and stop the clip. You can find video clips on the Internet, but remember that it is not permissible to tape a game and use it. If you wish, you might use a video clip of some other exciting event such as a car chase in a movie, as long as the event is short, exciting, and has a lot going on at once.

Procedure:

1. Show the video clip to the class—the clip should be no longer than a minute or two.

2. One student may volunteer or be selected to go to the screen and help direct the discussion of the events. She should challenge the others to find as many events as possible.

3. Each student will write down a description of what he has seen.

4. The students will discuss the clip. The teacher should encourage the students to be more specific about what happened. It may be appropriate to show the clip several more times before the students are able to discuss everything that happens.

5. The crucial point here is *everything*. The discussion should consider all the players on the field, off the field, the coaches, the fans, and anyone else who is involved in the event, including those at home watching the game. The point is to get the students to be as complete as possible in developing their description.

6. Students will pair off and start organizing a written discussion by listing events and discussing what emotions are displayed by various people involved in the event.

7. Students will write a description of the event, complete with some discussion of what, in their opinion, people are feeling during the play.

8. More advanced students may write a fictional account of one person who is seen in the event, describing how that person views what is going on and how that person feels about what is happening.

Evaluation: The object is to get students to write more completely by using a writing prompt which appeals to them.

Lesson 45
WEAVING A BOOK

Level: For middle school students and above (problem solving and review: for language arts)

Purpose: It can be hard for students to keep track of all of the complicated plot twists in a book together with all of the characters. This strategy is designed to help students *see* how the plot, subplots, and characters intertwine to result in the fabric of the book.

Time: This will take very little additional time for students as they read the story. The class exercise will depend on how much you want for the students to delve into the parts of the plot.

Materials:

- Colored sticky notes or colored paper dots
- Colored yarn or string; tape; a long surface on which you are allowed to use tape

Procedure:

1. Assign several students to keep track of the plot. As they read the book, they should make a timeline of the events. If there are subplots, students should be assigned to those as well. The remaining students should be assigned to keep track of individual characters, making timelines for them. As the students read the book, have the students in charge of the plots and subplots display the events in the classroom. This can be done on an unused blackboard or whiteboard, on a poster board, or on tape. If your school will allow, use painter's tape, which will come off without leaving marks. Use one strip of tape for the plot and one for each of the subplots. Assign each character a color, and put an appropriately colored dot or mark on the plot line each time a character appears in an event.

2. Each character will be assigned to a student or group of students, who will be given yarn of a particular color. Tape all the yarn at the beginning of the timeline, and start taping the yarn to the timeline at the points at which that character appears in each event. If a character is not involved, break that yarn, tape the end and then reconnect the appropriate yarn again when the character comes back into the story. If characters not involved in an event are later found to have been involved in something at some other location, sticky notes can be used to mark what happened in those subplots.

3. Have students see whose lines are most frequently attached, indicating that that character appears very often in the story. Identify characters who appear or disappear as the story proceeds. See how the plot and subplots, if any, interrelate, and how characters appear in both the main plot and subplots.

4. The first time that you do this, make sure that that you use a story with no flashbacks. As your students get more adept at weaving a story, you can include stories with more convoluted plot lines. The students should decide if they are going to display the plot as it appeared in time or as it appeared in the story.

Evaluation: This is intended to provide for your students a visual representation of the interrelationship of plot and characters. If your students have a clear understanding of how characters drive the plot and vice versa, this exercise is successful.

Students should be able to identify major characters—hero or heroine, protagonist, villain—as well as understanding how those individuals move the story along.

Lesson 46
WOD (WORD OF THE DAY)

Level: For all levels (enrichment: for all language-based courses)

Purpose: Some students have difficulty in expanding their vocabulary. This exercise is designed to allow students to learn new words by linking those words to information that they already have.

Time: Less than 5 minutes at the beginning of each class. If your classes are long (such as with a modified block schedule), you may want to have two Words of the Day.

Materials: Any source of words that are connected with material covered in class, including the textbook, magazines, other people (including teachers), or electronic sources

Procedure:

1. The students are to select any word that they find in an academic context that they don't know the meaning of or which they find interesting.

2. Once the word is selected, the student will look up the word in a dictionary to find:

   a. All the meanings of that word, particularly if the meanings do not appear to be related, such as the meanings of the word *interest*. As a noun, *interest* can mean "attention," "importance," "something you do for fun," or "the fee paid by a borrower to a lender." As a verb, *interest* means "to attract the attention of."

   b. The etymology of the word: where the word originated and what the original meaning of the word was. According to Merriam Webster's Dictionary, *interest* comes from the Latin word *interesse*, which means to be (*esse*) between (*inter*).

   c. The connotation and denotation of the word: What does the word imply? What is the literal meaning of the word? The denotation of the word is given by the definitions found in the dictionary. The connotation of *interest* can mean something more than just getting attention or being important. Said in one way, *interesting* can mean the exact opposite: Someone is telling you everything he did on his boring vacation. If you say "Interesting" without any emotion, you may mean that what happened was not interesting.

3. The student writes the word on the board in the place provided or displays the word in some way to the class. The student will have written the word, its etymology, and its meanings on a 3-by-5-inch card and will hand this in to the teacher.

4. When enough words have been accumulated, test the students' knowledge either in a paper-and-pencil test, a vocabulary "bee," or by giving them the list of words and having them use as many as they can in a story.

5. While this strategy is listed as a language arts strategy, it can be used in almost any class. You decide if you want to limit the words to those which relate to the material the class is studying or not.

Evaluation: The ultimate assessment occurs when students begin to use these words in their everyday life. However, you may also wish more traditional paper-and-pencil assessments, resulting in a grade.

4

Science

One of the authors of this book once surprised the students in her Advanced Placement psychology class a bit by coming in to class one day and announcing that the class was going to do a lab that involved the senses. One student said, "Are we really going to do something, or are you just going to show us?" The teacher pointed out that the only way they were really going to understand how they experience the world was to isolate each sense. When they actually located the blind spot in their visual field, many were astounded, because most people are totally unaware that what they actually see is not the smooth picture that their brain creates from the information. They were equally fascinated to find out how difficult it was to figure out what the smell is in a little unmarked bottle when there was no other information. The whole school was amused by the attempts of these students trying to throw and catch a ball when their peripheral vision was blocked by blinders and they could only see directly in front of them.

As a science teacher, this author has always felt that science can best be learned when students actively participate in what is being taught in class. If the only source of information is from the book or from the teacher, then what they are learning is history, because it is what has happened in the past. This is one of the reasons that active learners find science interesting and is probably one of the reasons that students who are more comfortable reading or listening find science less interesting.

This author once taught science in a girls' school, and had a very hard time at the beginning getting the girls to participate. In her coed AP psychology class, the girls will frequently pair up with boys and let them do

SCIENCE

the work while the girls take notes. She prevents that by pairing students up at random for each of the lab exercises done during the course. During the lab described above, most of the sections of the lab are to be done by both of the students so that the girls have to participate. One factor that should be taken into consideration is that research reveals that girls do better in the lab portion of a course when they have another girl for a lab partner (Ding & Harskamp, 2006).

Many students who are active learners tend to be impulsive and jump into the lesson before the teacher thinks they understand enough to do the exercise properly. Frequently, the teacher carefully goes over each step of the lab exercise so that all students fully comprehend exactly what they are to do to make sure that students are safe and that they learn from the lesson. The problem is that the active learner does not often listen and can become bored by the verbal description. When the students begin the exercise, that student has little information about what is to be done. This student is not likely to read a description of the lab the night before, either. What works better is to give a brief description of the lab—no more than 5 minutes. Do not talk about what the purpose of the lab is or what the students are to find out. That is for the discussion following the lab.

These steps will help integrate the active learner into a class with students who are good verbal and auditory learners:

1. If there is equipment which needs to be put together, have one setup for students to observe. Unless time is an issue, it is important for students to put the equipment together themselves and to put it away at the end of the lab. Make sure that the active learners are not always the ones who put the equipment together.

2. Provide detailed lab instruction sheets for students to follow. Break the lab into steps and number the steps on the sheet in bold type. When you give the brief introduction, point out each step by its title, but do not go too deeply into what students are to do. As they get used to the fact that you are not going to walk them through each step, they will learn to read more closely and start to figure out what they are to do. That "figuring out" process is the essence of science, and that is how students will learn to think like a scientist. Yes, I know that you want to make sure that they learn the material, but *they will learn it better if they figure it out than if you tell them.* It is very hard for many teachers to understand that some students do not learn from being told and have to experience for themselves.

3. For younger students, you can require the class to stop as they finish each step and then briefly point out what is going on in the next step. Once your students are familiar with the processes you use, you can just require that each group check with you before they move on to the next step without waiting for the entire class to be ready. That check may be nothing more than asking them what they are to do next. For older students, you can go over each step in the whole exercise and point out areas where they need to be careful. Yes, you will get a lot of questions asking what they are to do next. Direct them to read the lab directions and then tell you what they are to do next. This will seem frustrating at the beginning, but it will not be long before the students will start to depend on themselves and not

on the teacher. It is here that the experiential learners shine, as they usually have a good sense of how to do lab exercises.

4. As each group completes the lab, have them come to the board and list their data. Then they should clean up their material. When all the data is listed, ask the students what they learned from the lab. If they don't see the principles the lab exercise is demonstrating, don't tell them; instead, ask probing questions such as "Do you see any patterns in the results?" "What did you discover that surprised you?" and "What do you think the lab was about?"

5. All students should be required to write some summary of their experience. Younger students can draw a picture and label it to show what they did or write a brief statement about what they discovered. Older students can write a formal lab report.

It is important for students to actively be involved in science exercises. Doing something provides information which is far more complex than anything that can be gained by reading about what happens in a lab exercise. Not only does a student get an understanding of the complexity of how the world reacts, but she also begins the process of fitting information gained through experience into a theoretical framework. Without this ability, the student will not later be able to learn from experience and will see each event as a unique event without any connection to other events. Even for students who are not interested in science, the act of working through a lab exercise is crucial to developing the skills to be an independent learner. The world requires us to learn from what happens in our lives; without the training provided by the study of science, we would see each episode as totally new and unconnected to anything else in our lives. We would also not be able to decide what would happen if events were different—a skill that is essential in order for us to start to make reasoned decisions and control our impulses.

Interactive science lessons encourage students to

- become familiar with lab equipment and procedures,
- develop skills in observation and reporting, and
- understand that science is about what is happening in front of them.

Lesson 47
ANALYSIS OF BOLTS

Level: For middle school students (develops problem-solving skills and provides a lesson in collecting and manipulating data)

Purpose: To gain experience in measurement of mass and in calculating differences in measurements; to present students with real-life practical application of skills

Time: About 45 minutes

Materials: For each pair of students:

- 10 carriage bolts
- An electronic balance
- A calculator and a worksheet

Procedure:

1. Each pair of students should have 10 identical carriage bolts. These are readily available from any hardware store and can be reused for years. Any manufactured item will do as long as each item is easily measured on the balances available in the class—pieces of paper are too light. If your balance is sensitive enough, you can use paper clips.

2. Each student should measure each bolt, recording the mass in decigrams and in milligrams.

3. Using the worksheet, each student can then record the mass of each bolt and calculate the variation for the masses in both decigrams and milligrams.

4. For advanced students, the information can be used to calculate a *t*-test or a simple ANOVA.

Evaluation: Students will be able to discuss the metric system of mass, understanding the relationships among milligram, decigram, and gram. Students will be able to calculate variation and to demonstrate an understanding of the concept of how much difference is normal among similar items.

ANALYSIS OF BOLTS Worksheet

Name: _____

Procedure

1. Line up the 10 bolts and weigh each, recording the masses to the nearest decigram and to the nearest milligram.

2. Obtain the averages of the masses of the 10 bolts to the nearest decigram and to the nearest milligram.

3. Obtain the deviations from the average by subtracting each measurement from its average.

4. By examining the deviations, decide which method of measurement gives a more accurate description of the bolts.

Sample number	To the nearest decigram		To the nearest milligram	
	Mass in grams	Deviations in grams	Mass in grams	Deviations in grams
1				
2				
3				
4				
5				
6				
7				
8				
9				
10				
averages				

SCIENCE LESSONS

Questions

If you worked for the manufacturer and you know that your company does not do a good job, how could you report this data to make your company look good?

If you are in charge of making sure that your company does a good job of manufacturing these items, what would you do to make sure that your analysis of the items is accurate?

If you weigh one of these items, what will you learn and what will you not learn?

Lesson 48

HOW MANY CALORIES IN SUGARED CEREAL?

Warning: This lab involves hot water and burning food. Students should wear safety goggles and the student handling the flame should wear insulated gloves or be capable of managing tongs to manage the burning food.

Level: For upper-level students—lesson and incentive activity

Purpose: To connect the concept of heat gain to food by determining how many calories are in small bits of sugared cereal

Time: About 60 minutes

Materials: For each pair of students:

- A thermometer
- A 50-ml test tube and holder
- A 25-ml graduated cylinder
- An aluminum can, prepared as described below
- A cork with large pin stuck in it
- A balance
- Bits of sugared cereal (those with regular shapes such as loops or puffs will work better than flakes)

Procedure:

1. Use empty soda or pop cans for this apparatus. Cut the bottoms of the cans off and cut a large triangle out of the side to allow the food to be inserted. The can will look like this:

Calorimeter

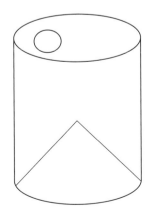

2. The traditional way to burn the food is to stick a pin through it and secure the pin to a cork with some space between the food and the cork. However, students may also use any heatproof surface that will fit inside the can, such as an overturned crucible. Make sure that the end of the test tube is about a centimeter or two above the cereal.

3. Students will need to figure out how to weigh the test tube with water in it. Since 1 ml of water is equivalent to 1 g, all they need to do is to weigh the empty test tube and be very careful about noting the amount of water that they put into the test tube.

4. You will be the best judge of whether or not to let your students set the cereal on fire or whether you should do it. However, they should think about why they do not want to light the cereal when it is inside the calorimeter, even though they will lose a bit of heat in transferring the cereal to the inside of the can once it is lit.

5. Once the cereal has finished burning, students should dump the remainder into a beaker of water to cool it off.

6. You may also supply other bits of food that are known to have high calories such as snack food, bits of bread, or potato chips. Be careful to select food that is fairly dry; chocolate, for example, takes a while to catch on fire.

Evaluation: Students will be able to calculate the number of calories given off by the combustion of food by determining the amount of heat transferred to water. Students will understand the concept of calories and how that relates to heat and energy.

HOW MANY CALORIES IN SUGARED CEREAL? Worksheet

Name: _____

Warning: This lab involves hot water and burning food. Students should wear safety goggles, and the student handling the flame should wear insulated gloves or be capable of managing tongs to manage the burning food.

Procedure

1. You will be given a calorimetry apparatus consisting of a 50-ml test tube and a soda or pop can modified for this experiment. The purpose of the can is to make sure that as much heat from the cereal goes to heat the water as is possible.

2. You need to weigh the empty test tube and secure it in such a way that the bottom goes through the hole at the top of the can and stops about 1 to 2 centimeters above where your cereal will be.

3. Put 20 ml of water in the test tube. You need to be very accurate as you cannot directly mass the test tube with the water in it. 1 ml of water is equivalent to 1 g of water. Use that equivalency to determine what the mass of the test tube and water is. Put a thermometer in the test tube.

4. Select a bit of sugared cereal. Prepare it for this operation as directed by your teacher. You will either be putting a pin through the cereal and sticking the pin in a cork (leaving some space between the cork and the cereal) or placing the cereal on a heat-proof device.

5. Take the temperature of the water in the test tube.

6. One partner will hold the thermometer and stir it *gently* as the cereal burns. The other partner either lights the cereal or asks the teacher to light the cereal. Once the cereal is lit, it should be immediately placed inside the calorimetry apparatus.

7. The partner with the thermometer notes the rising temperature and reads the maximum temperature reached by the water.

8. This operation will be repeated with fresh water and a new piece of cereal.

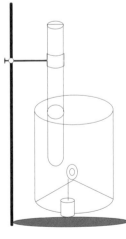

SCIENCE LESSONS

9. Data:

		Trial 1	Trial 2
Mass of test tube and water	g		
Mass of empty test tube	g		
Mass of water (m_w)	g		
Final temperature (t_f)	°C		
Initial temperature (t_i)	°C		
Change in temperature	°C		
Heat gained (H+)	cal		

10. Calculate heat gained:

$$H+ = m_w \times (t_f - t_i)$$

11. Graph time and heat gained.

Questions

1. How many calories did you determine there were in your bit of cereal?

2. How many calories are there supposed to be in a serving of your cereal (as stated on the side of the box)? So how many bits of cereal would there be in one serving?

Lesson 49

HOW A CANDLE BURNS

Warning: This lesson involves open flames.

Level: For middle school students and above (lesson and incentive activity)

Purpose: To gain experience in timekeeping and in metric measurement of length; to practice plotting points, making a line graph, and reporting results of an experiment

Time: About 45 minutes

Materials: For each pair of students:

- A birthday candle
- A small block of wood
- A metric ruler
- Matches or a fireplace lighter
- A timekeeping device capable of measuring minutes to the nearest second
- The accompanying worksheet and graph paper

Procedure:

1. Before the lab begins, light one candle and drip a few drops of melted wax on one of the blocks. Immediately stick another candle into the wax and hold for a few seconds until the wax hardens enough to hold the candle upright. Make sure that the candle is near an edge of the block as it will make it easier for the students to measure. Do not use a candle to supply its own wax as that will diminish the candle and it may not last the whole time.

2. Give each pair of students a candle with its attached block, a ruler, and a timekeeping device.

3. Direct the students to measure the length of the candle before it is lit. Make sure that the students understand that the end of a ruler is not to be trusted and that they should start measuring further up the ruler.

4. Tell the students that they will light the candle, let it burn for one minute, then blow it out and measure its length. They will then relight the candle, blow it out again after a minute, and measure again. They will continue this process until the candle has been lit 10 times. Show them how to use the worksheet to mark down the data.

5. Once the data has been collected, show the students how to graph the data. Do not explain this beforehand, as the active learners may not remember. Point out that a graph needs to reflect the data collected as well as the experience in the lab. Once all students have graphed the data by hand, you may want to show them how to use a computer program to graph as well.

6. This is a simple lab with very clear results and can be used as the basis for writing a lab report. Each teacher will have a different form to use, but be clear exactly what your expectations are concerning what you want in the finished product.

7. Demonstration: If you have time, you may want to light a candle and let it burn until it burns out. That will take much less than 10 minutes. Ask the students why their candles lasted for 10 minutes and yours did not.

Evaluation: Students will be able to discuss the metric system of measuring length and to use a graph to explain the results of the experiment. Students will be able to write a coherent explanation of what they did, what happened, and what information they learned from the exercise.

HOW A CANDLE BURNS Worksheet

Name: _____

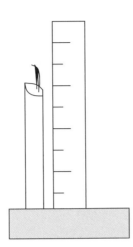

Data Table:

Elapsed time in minutes	Height of candle in centimeters
0	
1	
2	
3	
4	
5	
6	
7	
8	
9	
10	
Average loss of wax per minute	

Lesson 50

CHANGE OF STATES OF MATTER

Level: For elementary to middle school students (lesson)

Purpose: To gain experience in lab techniques; to develop an understanding for what happens to matter when there is a change of state

Time: About 45 minutes

Materials: For each pair of students:

- A small plastic jar with tight-fitting lid
- Ice; salt; water
- An electronic balance

For advanced students

- Safety goggles
- One eighth of an Alka-Seltzer tablet

Procedure:

1. Each pair of students will weigh the small jar together with its lid and record the mass on the worksheet in the appropriate area.

2. Each group will obtain a small amount of crushed ice, put it in the jar, put the lid on tightly, and weigh the jar with its contents.

3. Students can encourage melting of the ice by shaking the jar, holding it in their hands, or putting the jar in a sunny window. This is an excellent place to discuss what is needed to freeze or melt water.

4. Once the ice is melted, students should weigh the jar and contents again and note any difference in mass.

5. Point out that the solid is now a liquid, and ask them what happened to the mass of their ice (now water). Point out that one usually thinks of solids as weighing more than liquids, and then ask them why there was no loss of mass. Don't tell the students; help them figure out that even though the substance was once a solid and is now a liquid, nothing has been added or taken away from the jar, so the mass remains the same.

6. Have the students empty and dry out the jars, then fill each jar about half full of water. Put a small amount of salt on each lid and have the students weigh the jar with water and the lid with salt together. You will need to discover before the lab approximately how much salt should be given to the students so that when they mix it into the water all the salt will dissolve.

7. Have the students pour the salt very carefully into the water in the jar, put the lid on tightly, and shake the contents to dissolve the salt. The students

can perform this operation over a piece of paper so that if any salt spills it can be recovered. When they shake the jars, make sure that they hold the lid tightly to make sure nothing spills out.

8. Once the salt has dissolved, students should then weigh the jar and contents again and note any difference in mass.

9. Point out that the salt has disappeared and ask them what happened to the mass of their mixture. Ask them why there was no loss in mass even though the salt disappeared.

For advanced students

10. Do the same process with the small bit of Alka-Seltzer tablet. Before students are given this task, try the exercise yourself to make sure that the bottle and lid will take the pressure from the released gas. There are bottles available from science supply houses for this purpose, but a small amount of tablet should not cause a problem. The major source of error in this lab occurs when students do not get the lid on quickly enough or tightly enough. Direct students to listen to the bottle carefully to see if they can detect escaping gas.

11. Have the students pour the water into the jar, place the tablet on the lid, and weigh the jar and the lid together. Make sure that the inside of the lid is very dry, or the tablet will begin dissolving too soon. Students should drop the bit of tablet into the water, immediately put the lid on, and tighten it completely. They should observe the change that takes place within the jar.

12. Once the tablet has totally dissolved, have the students weigh the jar with the lid on, then remove the lid and weight the jar and lid again. The difference in mass will be the mass of the gas released by the tablet.

13. Ask them why there was a significant difference in mass after the lid was removed. Ask them why their results were different this time from the first two times.

Evaluation: Students will be able to discuss the principle of change of state of matter, pointing out that even though matter has changed its state, if no material escapes from the jar, no matter has been lost.

CHANGE OF STATES OF MATTER Worksheet

Name: _____

Part 1: Solid to liquid

	Mass of container	Mass of container and contents	Mass of contents
Before melting			
After melting			
		Difference:	

1. What happened to the ice in the container from the start to the finish?

2. How did you know that a change had taken place?

3. Was there a significant difference in the mass of the contents from the start to the finish of the exercise?

Part 2: Dissolving

	Mass of container	Mass of container and contents	Mass of contents
Before melting			
After melting			
		Difference:	

1. What happened to the salt once it was put in the water in the container?

2. How did you know a change had taken place?

3. Was there a significant difference between the mass of the contents before and after mixing? If there was, how could you account for the difference?

For Advanced Students:

Put on safety goggles before you begin this part of the lab.

Solid to gas

	Mass of container	Mass of container and contents	Mass of contents
Before mixing			
After mixing			
After lid removed			
		Difference from first mass to last:	

1. What did the Alka-Seltzer tablet look like before mixing?

2. What did the tablet look like after mixing?

3. How did you know that a change had taken place?

4. Was there a significant difference from the first mass to the last?

5. How can you account for that difference?

6. What was the mass of the gas?

Lesson 51
COLORS!

Level: For middle school students and above (enrichment and problem-solving skills)

Purpose: To experience the science of dyeing fabric; to try out various sources of colors; to see where color comes from; to develop an understanding of the chemistry of dye

Time: Several sessions, about 30 to 45 minutes each time

Materials:

- Rubber gloves (kitchen type, not sterile gloves); waterproof aprons
- Various sources of natural dyes: beets, onion skins, grass, carrots, blueberries, coffee, tea, red cabbage, red clays (soil), and turmeric are a few natural sources. Other sources of dyes are powdered drink mixes or food colors.
- Squares of cotton fabric (old sheets work well as long as they are cotton)
- Containers to dye fabric in (these should not be used to prepare food in)
- Hot plate

For older students:

- Different types of fabric
- Salt; alum; cream of tartar

Sources for materials: Ground turmeric is a spice found with the rest of the spices in the grocery store. Cream of tartar will be found in the same location. Alum can be found in the grocery store with supplies for making pickles or in a pharmacy.

Procedure:

For younger students

1. Have each group of students select a source of color. They should examine the source and determine what the color should look like before beginning.

2. Have students prepare their substance for dyeing. They will need to wear the gloves and aprons to protect themselves. The outside brown part of onions should be put in water and gently boiled (simmered) for 30 minutes before being used. The other sources should be crushed in water to release the color and the liquid heated. Before putting the fabric in the dye, you may have students strain the liquids to remove the coloring matter.

3. The squares of cotton fabric should be washed well before using. Have the students wet the fabric before putting it in the dye. If possible, students should have several different squares.

a. The squares can be left in the dye for different amounts of time.

b. The dye can be heated (not boiled) while some of the squares are in the liquid.

4. The squares should be put out on paper towels to dry.

5. Students can compare the colors they have obtained from the various sources.

a. They can leave some squares in the sun and put others into a covered container. After a week, they can compare the squares.

b. They can wash some squares in plain water and others in detergent and compare the squares.

For older students

6. Follow the procedure for younger students, but include different types of fabric. Make sure that all the fabric is either natural color or bleached and wash all fabric before using. The types of fabric that can be used are silk, linen, wool, rayon, polyester, and blends of fabrics, as well as different weights of cotton fabric such as muslin, canvas, and twill.

7. Have the students make hypotheses about their dye and fabric based on research done before beginning the exercise.

8. The squares of fabric should be wet before being added to the dye and should be heated in the dye for at least 30 minutes to insure good absorption of the dye.

9. A *mordant* is a substance added to dye to make the color more permanent. Prepare a mordant made of three parts alum to one part cream of tartar for the students to use. Students can also try using salt as a mordant and comparing the results.

10. For dye that is intended to be permanent, students should add the mordant to the dye water before adding the squares of fabric and then simmer the fabric in the dye and mordant for a half an hour.

11. Squares should be dried on paper towels.

12. Students can compare the squares of fabric according to the type of fabric and the dye. They can also test for colorfastness according to fabric, dye, source of color, and mordant used. Students might also try dyeing fabric in several different dyes to see what happens to the color.

13. You can invite a batik artist in to the classroom to demonstrate those techniques.

Evaluation: Students will demonstrate an understanding of color sources and the principles of water-soluble dyeing. Students will be able to explain what a mordant is and how it makes dyes colorfast.

Lesson 52
HOT WATER

Warning: This lab involves hot water and a heat source. Students should wear safety goggles, and the student handling the beaker should wear insulated gloves or be capable of managing tongs to remove a hot beaker from the heat source.

Level: For upper-level students—lesson and alternative modality

Purpose: To introduce the concept of heat gain as measured in calories; to provide experience in working with calorimetry

Time: About 60 minutes

Materials: For each pair of students:

- Scientific thermometer
- 100 ml beaker
- Balance
- Heat source such as a hot plate
- An insulated glove or tongs to remove the beaker from the heat source

Procedure:

1. Turn on the heat sources to allow them to come to the appropriate temperature of 100°C.

2. Direct the students to mass the empty beakers. They will not need to reweigh the beaker even it if has water left from a previous trial as long as the outside is dry. Students should be able to figure out why this is true.

3. Students will fill the beaker half full of tap water, then weigh the beaker and water.

4. They will put the thermometer in the water, then read the temperature once the thermometer has adjusted to the water.

5. One student will put the beaker on the heat source and *gently* stir the thermometer.

6. When the time is up, the student will remove the beaker and immediately read the thermometer.

7. The water will be poured out, fresh water put into the beaker, and the process repeated two more times with increasing time intervals.

Evaluation: Students will be able to discuss the concepts of heat gain, calories, and convection. Students will be able to calculate heat gained from the change in temperature and should be able to determine the beginning temperature given final temperature and heat gain.

HOT WATER Worksheet

Name: _____

Warning: This lab involves hot water and a heat source. Students should wear safety goggles, and the student handling the beaker should wear insulated gloves or be capable of managing tongs to remove a hot beaker from the heat source.

Procedure

1. Mass the empty beakers and record that mass on the table. That mass will not change unless the outside of the beaker gets wet.

2. Fill the beaker about half full of water, then weigh the beaker and water together.

3. Put the thermometer in the water, allow it to adjust to the temperature of the water, and note that value on the table.

4. One partner will be the timekeeper. The other partner will put the beaker on the heat source and *gently* stir with the thermometer. When 30 seconds are up, the timekeeper will inform the other partner, who will safely remove the beaker from the heat source and immediately read the thermometer.

5. Empty the water from the beaker and refill the beaker about half full with tap water.

6. Repeat the procedure using 50 seconds for the second trial, and 70 seconds for the third trial.

7. Data:

		Trial 1	Trial 2	Trial 3
Mass of beaker and water	g			
Mass of empty beaker	g			
Mass of water (m_w)	g			
Heating time	sec			
Final temperature (t_f)	°C			
Initial temperature (t_i)	°C			
Change in temperature	°C			
Heat gained (H+)	cal			

8. Calculate heat gained:

$$H+ = m_w \times (t_f - t_i)$$

9. Graph time and heat gained.

Questions

1. From the direction of the graph, what appears to be the mathematical nature of the relationship between heat development and the passage of time?

2. Does it appear that the heat source converts electrical energy into thermal energy at a constant or uniform rate?

   Can you determine what the rate is?

3. Why did we not need to use the same amount of water in each trial?

Lesson 53
I SPY

Level: Can be adapted for all levels (problem-solving skills)

Purpose: To gain experience in developing skills in observation, to become familiar with common insects and other environmental matter

Time: About 45 minutes

Materials: For each student:

- Four large paper clips; string; magnifying glass
- For the inside version: one half meter of masking tape
- For older students: swabs and Petri dishes with agar

Procedure:

1. Each student will pick a location outside to examine. Straighten the outside loop of each paper clip so that the clip can be stuck into the ground and the small loop will be available to hold the string.

   Mark off a square for each student. The area should be around 1/2 meter square for younger students and 1 meter square for older students. Stick the paper clips in each corner of the square and run string through the loops to mark off the area.

2. Once the areas are marked off, the students will carefully examine every single thing that is in the square: all living things will be noted, described, and a picture drawn. These can include animals such as insects and plants such as grass. All non-living items will be noted and described; this may include trash and rocks. The examination will require use of a magnifying glass.

3. If an outdoor location is not available or not practical, each student will obtain a length of masking tape, stick it to a location, then quickly and carefully pull the tape away. The tape will be used on surfaces only, not on people or other living creatures. Glass is not a good choice as it may be difficult to remove the tape from that surface.

4. Once the tape is removed, students will turn it over and carefully examine all the material that was picked up by the tape, describing the material and making hypotheses about the source of such material.

5. Older students will look at their areas more carefully by swabbing the area and transferring that to the agar in the Petri dish. The dishes should be taped shut and left for two days. If you have an incubator, you may use that, but simply putting the dishes in a warm dark location will be enough. Students will examine the dishes without opening them, describing the

kinds of colonies which have grown in the dish. If you have the proper equipment to allow students to extract material from the dishes, they may examine the material in the colonies under a microscope. If you do not have this equipment, do not allow the students to open the Petri dishes, but discard them in a safe location.

Evaluation: Students will gain an understanding of what small creatures are around us and be able to describe them. Students will gain skills in observation and in record keeping.

Lesson 54

HOW MUCH DOES YOUR STATE WEIGH?

Topic: For middle-school students and above (enrichment and incentive activity)

Purpose: To gain experience in measurement of area and mass; to be able to use ratio and proportion to develop information; to understand scale differences

Time: About 60 minutes

Materials: For each pair of students:

- A sheet of paper with a line map printed on it
- A pair of scissors; a ruler; an electronic balance; a calculator
- Worksheet

Procedure:

1. There are two different levels of this lab; be sure to select the one appropriate for your students.

2. Each student will determine the length and width of the piece of paper as well as the mass of the paper.

3. Each student will calculate the area of the paper.

4. The students should carefully cut out the map from the piece of paper and weigh the map as well as the left over pieces of paper. The students will ascertain that they have all of the paper accounted for by adding together the weights of the map the leftover pieces.

5. Using the formula on the worksheet, students will calculate the area of the map.

6. Students will compare the calculated area of the map with information from an atlas or from the Internet and determine what difference exists between calculated area and accepted area.

Evaluation: Students will be able to discuss the metric system of measuring length, area, and mass. Students will demonstrate understanding of the relationship between scale measurement and actual measurement.

Sources of maps: You will find state maps at www.eduplace.com. Click on Outline Maps at the bottom of the home page, then click on United States, then click on State Maps, then select the appropriate map. You will need an atlas to calculate the scale of the map as these maps are not all drawn to the same scale.

1. Copy the state map of your choosing and measure a straight side.

2. Measure the same side on the map in the atlas.

3. Determine the length of that side in miles using the scale on the map in the atlas.

4. That side on the small map is equivalent to the length in miles that you calculated in Step 3. Divide the miles by the length in centimeters that you calculated in Step 1, and you have your scale.

5. For example, the selected side on the map in the atlas is 15.5 centimeters. According to the scale in the atlas, 2.3 cm is equivalent to 10 miles. So 15.5 centimeters is equal to 67.3 miles. The same portion on the small map is 4.7 cm. That means that the 4.7cm on the small map is also equal to 67.3 miles, so the scale on the small map is 67.3 miles/4.7 cm or 14.3 miles. 1 cm = 14.3 miles.

HOW MUCH DOES YOUR STATE WEIGH? Worksheet

Name: _____

Data

1. Total area of paper map is printed on:
   a. Length _____
   b. Width _____
   c. Area _____

2. Mass of paper map is printed on: _____

3. Cut map out and obtain the mass of just the map: _____

4. Mass of paper left over from cutting out map: _____

5. Calculate difference: Mass of (1) − [mass of (3) + mass of (4)]:
   _____

6. Calculate percentage difference: (Difference/expected) × 100:
   _____

Establishment of Equivalent Ratios

7. Find the scale of your map.

8. Calculate what 1 cm^2 of your map is equivalent to in miles^2: If 1 cm on map equals 60 miles, then 1cm^2 = 3,600 miles^2. Be careful: It is squared, not multiplied by 2.

9. Calculate the total number of square miles the whole piece of paper is equivalent to: Multiply the scale of the map (7) by the equivalence in miles^2 (8).

10. What percent of the total paper is the map? Divide the mass of the map (4) by the mass of the total paper (2).

11. What is the area of the map? Multiply the total number of square miles in the whole piece of paper obtained in (9) by the percent obtained in (10).

(Advanced students)

12. Find the area of the state you are measuring.

13. What is the difference between the figure you obtained and the actual area? Is that a significant difference (more than 5%)?

14. If the difference in (5) above is greater than 5%, adjust the final area of your state by the percent difference. Does this get you closer to the expected value for the area of the state?

15. What are some of the reasons that you may not have gotten a very accurate result when you calculated the area using this method? Be specific.

Lesson 55
PUT IT TOGETHER

Level: Can be adapted for all levels (review and alternative modality: can be used for any appropriate lesson)

Purpose: To develop an understanding of how various systems work by actively participating in creating a model of that system

Time: About 60 minutes per exercise

Materials: Some method of randomly assigning students to groups or positions

Procedure: There are several different versions of this exercise. Each is described, and the teacher will select which version suits the class. If there are more students than roles, they can double up, or there may be enough students for two complete versions.

1. *Build a cell:* List all of the various organelles in a cell, and choose whether the cell will be from a plant or an animal. Each student will be assigned to be responsible for one organelle and will be given time to become familiar with the role of that organelle. Several students may work together as the cell wall or cell membrane. Tell the students that they are to function saying out loud what they are doing in the life of the cell. Then they will be asked to build a protein and each organelle (student) must then say how they fit into the production of the protein.

   For younger students: Make paper rings to fit around the top of student's heads and put on the front a card with either the name of a part of a cell or a picture of that part. Students will not be able to see what they are, but must ask questions of other students about what their function is to guess what part of the cell they are. They may not ask directly what part of the cell they have been assigned.

2. *Build an atom:* Have students draw slips on which are written either *P*, *N*, or *E*—standing for *proton, neutron,* or *electron*. Students can pin those letters to themselves so that others can see who they are. Then tell the students to make atoms with the appropriate number of elements. Ask the class to make the biggest atom they can with the particles they have, name that atom, then make the smallest atoms they can using all of the elements—no proton/electron duos claiming to be hydrogen atoms should be allowed unless all the neutrons have been included in atoms.

   For advanced students: Have them make compounds using several atoms. Use different colored yarn to represent different types of chemical bonds and have the students include the correct bond in the compound. Have students represent ions and radioactive atoms.

3. *Build a circuit:* Have students draw slips which have various parts of an electrical circuit on them: battery, wire, light bulb, switch, and so forth.

SCIENCE LESSONS

Students selected as batteries must mark one hand as positive and the other as negative. Students will then join hands appropriately to make a circuit. One student who is not in the circuit will then trace the path to make sure that the circuit will work and draw that on the board. Then the class will attempt to make that circuit with electrical equipment to double check that it works.

Evaluation: These exercises are intended to give students a review of material they have already covered. Good understanding of the material will be reflected in assessments.

Lesson 56

RATIO OF SURFACE AREA TO VOLUME

Level: For students familiar with ratio and proportion (review and alternative modality)

Purpose: To demonstrate the relationship between surface area and volume; to introduce the concept of the change in ratio as the values involved change; to practice determining volume by different means

Time: About 45 minutes

Materials:

- A volume set—clear containers in the shapes of cubes, rectangles, cylinders, cone, and pyramids
- Rulers; triangles
- 100-ml and 10-ml graduated cylinders

Procedure:

1. Read with the students the first part of the worksheet. Point out that the first two rows in the first chart describe what they are to measure.

2. Direct the students to complete the chart on their own.

3. Once a pair of students has completed the table, set them to work on the second portion of the lab. They should be able to read the directions and determine the volume both by calculating and by pouring water into the shape. Then they must decide which of their measurements is more likely to be accurate and use that as the standard by which to determine the percentage difference.

4. Each pair should then figure out the surface area of the shape. Then they will calculate the ratio of surface area to volume.

5. As the students calculate the ratio of surface area to volume, they should post their results on the board. Once all are complete, students should discuss the effects of surface area cooling and heating.

Evaluation: Students will be able to determine the volume for various shapes, to determine the surface area for various shapes, and to calculate the ratio of volume to surface area. They will understand the principle of surface area and how it affects various properties.

Formulas:

Volume of a cone: $1/3\ \pi r^2 h$

Volume of a right pyramid: $1/3\ (lwh)$

Volume of a cylinder: $\pi r^2 h$

Surface area of a cone = slant height πr

THE RATIO OF SURFACE AREA TO VOLUME Worksheet

Name: _____

Procedure

1. A cube has six faces, so its total surface area is six times the area of one of its faces. It follows that the surface of a cube whose edges are 1 cm in length is the area of one face (1 cm^2) times 6, which equals 6 cm^2, while its volume is 1cm $\times$ 1 cm $\times$ 1cm or 1 cm^3.

2. The surface of a cube whose edges are 2 cm in length is (2 cm $\times$ 2 cm) $\times$ 6 or 24 cm^2, while its volume is 2 cm $\times$ 2 cm $\times$ 2 cm or 8 cm^3.

3. Work out and enter values for the remaining eight lines.

4. Divide the surface area by the volume to get the ratio.

Edge length (cm)	Total surface area	Volume of the cube	Ratio of total surface to volume
1	*6 cm²*	*1 cm³*	*6:1*
2	*24 cm²*	*8 cm³*	*24:8 or 3:1*
3			
4			
5			
6			
7			
8			
9			
10			

5. In the second part of this exercise, you are to determine the volume of two of the clear shapes, then fill them with water and determine how close you came to the expected volume by comparing the calculated volume with the liquid volume.

Shape of figure	Calculated volume	Liquid volume	Difference	Percentage difference

Now, determine the ratio of total surface area to volume for one of your figures.

Shape of figure: _____

Total surface area: _____

Volume of figure: _____

Ratio of area to volume: _____

Questions

1. Which shape has the highest ratio of surface area to volume? Which has the lowest?

2. Explain why your lungs are spongelike and not balloonlike if the point is to be able to have lots of surface area for the oxygen to move into your blood stream.

3. What shape house would be the best at holding heat in? What shape house would be the best at getting rid of heat in the summertime?

Lesson 57

DENSITY OF SOLIDS

Level: Beginning lesson in density (lesson and alternative modality)

Purpose: To give students experience in determining density of both regular and irregular solids

Time: About 60 minutes, or two 40-minute sessions if you do the determination of density of regular solids in one session and density of irregular solids in another

Materials: For each pair of students:

- 100-ml graduated cylinder
- Regularly shaped objects such as wooden blocks, sponges, and pieces of toys (do not use cylinders or spheres unless your students are familiar with the math of determining volume of such objects)
- Irregularly shaped objects that will not float and will fit within the graduated cylinder, such as small rocks, cylinder masses from a set, or other items in a lab
- A ruler
- A balance

Procedure:

1. Each pair of students begins by selecting a regularly shaped object. They are to complete collecting data according to the sheet. They will sketch their object, labeling the lengths of each side.

2. They will determine the volume of the object, mass it, and determine the density of the object.

3. Students can do two different objects if time allows.

4. Students will then move to select an irregularly shaped object. They will mass it and will determine volume by water displacement. Make sure that students understand that they are to slide the objects into the graduated cylinders. If the objects are dropped in, the water may splash out, compromising their measurements. Discuss with students the relationship between cubic centimeters and milliliters.

5. Using mass and volume, students are to determine the density of their object.

6. Students should compare data and see if there are any objects with similar densities.

Evaluation: Students will be able to describe the relationship between volume and mass in determining density. They will understand the difference between mass and density.

THE DENSITY OF SOLIDS Worksheet

Name: _____

Regular objects

1. Sketch your object and label all sides:

2. Formula used in calculating volume:

3. Volume of object (in cm^3):

4. Mass of object (in grams):

5. Density of Object:

   D = _____g

   _____cm^3

Irregularly shaped objects

1. Sketch of your object:

2. Mass of object (in grams):

3. Volume of object: Put 50 ml of water in the graduated cylinder, then gently slide the object into the cylinder. Determine the volume of water and object. Subtract to get the volume of the object:

   Volume of water and object: _____ml

   Starting volume: <u>50 ml</u>

   Volume of object alone: _____ml

4. Calculate density of object:

Questions

1. Why was it more difficult to determine the density of an irregularly shaped object than the density of a regular object?

2. What is the difference between mass and density?

3. Why must the irregularly shaped object not float?

4. How could you determine the density of an irregularly shaped object that floats, such as a natural sponge or a plastic toy building block?

Lesson 58
DENSITY OF LIQUIDS

Level: For students familiar with density (lesson and alternative modality)

Purpose: To give students practice in determining density of liquids and comparing the density of various liquids

Time: About 60 minutes

Materials:

- 10-ml graduated cylinder
- Balance
- Hydrometers, if available, for advanced students (will need 100-ml graduated cylinders)
- Liquids

  o Tap water
  o Distilled water
  o Saturated solution of salt and water
  o Cooking oil
  o "Heavy" mineral oil (get at pharmacy)
  o Rubbing alcohol
  o Mouthwash

Procedure:

1. Review with students the principles of density and what information is necessary to determine density. Brainstorm with them about how they would determine mass and volume of liquids. Remind them of the connection between milliliters and cubic centimeters.

2. Introduce the various liquids to them and have them decide which liquids they think will be denser and which will be less dense. *Do not help them make these decisions.* The point of lab exercises for experiential learners is to experience the lab for themselves. If they are incorrect, that is just fine; the lab exercise will correct them.

3. All students should weigh their graduated cylinder first while it is dry and clean. Discuss the problems in reusing the cylinder and what they will have to do to make sure each time that the data they collect is correct. They need to clean and dry the cylinder after each use.

4. Have students complete the sheet, collecting the data. Make sure that they know to do the oils last and use soap and water to rinse the oil out of the cylinders.

5. Compare data and ask again which liquids are more dense and which less dense. Discuss why this might be true. Point out the problems of oil spills in salt water.

6. If you have time, put a bit of food coloring in several of the liquids and pour 10 ml of each carefully one at a time into a 100-ml graduated cylinder, in order from the most dense to the least dense. With practice, you should be able to layer the liquids. Food coloring will not work in the oils, but they are generally somewhat naturally colored.

7. With a more advanced class, introduce the hydrometers and recalculate the densities of the liquids.

Evaluation: Students will be able to calculate the density of a variety of liquids and will understand the relationship between volume, mass, and density. Students will be able to describe the effect of various substances on the density of liquids.

DENSITY OF LIQUIDS Worksheet

Name: _____

Name of liquid	Mass of liquid in cylinder	Mass of cylinder	Mass of liquid	Volume of liquid	Density of liquid

Lesson 59

THICKNESS OF ALUMINUM FOIL

Level: For students familiar with density (enrichment and problem solving)

Purpose: To give students practice in using density to find other values; to engage students in practical application of new knowledge

Time: About 60 minutes

Materials:

- Ruler; balance; calculator
- Small squares of different types of aluminum foil
- Digital micrometer (optional)

Procedure:

1. Students should be familiar with the concept of density before beginning this exercise.

2. The density of aluminum is 2.7g/cm^3. Students should know that they will be able to determine the length, width, and mass of each piece and that they will be missing the height or thickness of the foil.

3. Before the exercise, cut various types and thicknesses of aluminum foil into small squares, approximately 4 cm by 4 cm. You might use a generic foil, a name brand foil, and a heavy-duty name brand foil. There is no need to get the measurements exact as the students will measure the squares, but you should attempt to get the pieces square. Cutting thin, inexpensive aluminum foil so that the pieces stay smooth can be difficult, but try using sharp scissors.

4. Students will be directed to measure the length and width of their pieces of foil and then obtain the mass of each piece. The numbers in this exercise are very small, so accuracy can make a big difference.

5. Students will then calculate the thickness of each piece of foil.

6. If you have a digital micrometer available, you can use that to check the students' values.

Evaluation: Students will be able to use formulas to acquire information that may not be readily available using information that is available. Students will get practice in obtaining measurements and in calculating values. Students will become familiar with the concept of density.

THE THICKNESS OF ALUMINUM FOIL Worksheet

Name: _____

Directions

1. Obtain three squares of three different varieties of aluminum foil. Be careful to keep the squares smooth.

2. Measure the length and width of the square of foil, then obtain the mass of the square and enter the data in the table.

3. Using the density of aluminum of 2.7 g/cm^3, figure out the thickness of each piece of foil.

	Generic foil	Name brand foil	Heavy duty foil
Dimensions of foil			
Area of square			
Mass of square			
Volume of square			
Height of square			

4. Remember $D = V/M$. You have been given the value of D, density. You have determined the mass (M) of the piece, and you have two of the three measurements to determine V, volume—length and width. What you are missing is height.

5. Use the mass and density to determine the volume of the square.

6. Use the length, width, and volume to determine the height or thickness of the square.

Questions

1. Were the pieces of foil all the same size?

   a. Should that make a difference in your calculations?

2. Was there a difference in thickness among the foils?

   a. Can you feel a difference with your fingers?

   b. Why might you have a hard time finding that difference?

3. Suppose you have a shallow pan that measures 20 cm by 25 cm and is filled with one layer of cubic building blocks that are 1 cm on a side. How many blocks are in the pan?

   a. If the total mass of the blocks is 325 g, how much does one block weigh?

4. The density of copper is 8.9 g/cm^3. If you have a cube of copper that is 2 cm on a side, how heavy is that cube of copper?

Lesson 60

VOLUME OF A LIQUID

Level: Introductory lesson in lab equipment (problem solving and alternative modality)

Purpose: To develop skills in managing laboratory equipment; to understand principles of liquids

Time: About 30 minutes

Materials:

- 10-ml graduated cylinder
- 50-ml graduated cylinder
- Medicine dropper
- Other small containers such as small beakers (50 or 100 ml), test tubes (with a holder), empty soda bottles, coffee mugs, plastic storage containers, or anything else that is available
- Water; salt; dish detergent
- Worksheet

Procedure:

1. Before the exercise, prepare solutions of salty water and soapy water. Dissolve as much salt as you can in room temperature water. When preparing the soapy water, take care not to let it get too foamy, but do put enough detergent in to make the water feel slippery.

2. Introduce students to the exercise by identifying all of the materials. Make sure that all students have access to the graduated cylinders and a medicine dropper.

3. Ask students to look at the graduated cylinders and to describe what the marks on the side of the cylinder mean. Do not tell them; have them figure it out.
   a. What does *ml* mean?
   b. Why are some lines longer than others?
   c. What is the total volume that can be measured by your cylinder?

4. Have students put some water in the 10-ml cylinder, not up to the top, and read the volume in the cylinder. Ask students what the problem is in reading the volume accurately.

5. Draw a section of a cylinder on the board and ask a student to come up and draw what she or he sees in the cylinder. Students will have a hard time doing this because of the meniscus. The meniscus is formed when water climbs up the side of the cylinder; it will be larger in the narrower containers and in glass containers. For older students, explain capillary action. Because students are viewing the column of water through the side, it is

SCIENCE LESSONS

hard to determine where the top of the water is. Tell the students to read the level of water at the bottom of the meniscus.

6. Have the students complete the accompanying worksheet, working independently.

7. After all students have completed the tasks and put away the equipment, discuss with the students the principles of measuring liquids and how salt and soap change the quality of water.

8. If you have time, you may have students measure other liquids such as sports drinks, coffee, mouthwash, and the like. You can also demonstrate to the students the measurement of cooking oil with a medicine dropper and cylinder dedicated to the task.

Evaluation: Students will be able to discuss the metric system of measuring volume and have some understanding of how much 10 ml is and what 1 liter is. Students will be able to explain how salt and soap change the quality of water so that measurements are different.

THE VOLUME OF A LIQUID Worksheet

Name: _____

Measurement of Plain Water

Equipment item— cylinders and other containers	Rated size of container	Capacity of container filled to rim

Plain Water

1. Put 9 ml of water in the 10-ml graduated cylinder. How many drops of water are necessary to raise the level of water to 10 ml?

   _____

2. Put 10 ml of water in the 10-ml graduated cylinder. Pour that into an empty 50-ml cylinder.

3. What is the level of the liquid in the larger cylinder?

   _____

4. How many times are necessary to pour 10 ml of water into the 50-ml cylinder to exactly reach the 50 ml mark? _____

SCIENCE LESSONS

Salty Water

1. Put 9 ml of water in the 10-ml graduated cylinder. How many drops of water are necessary to raise the level of water to 10 ml? _____

2. Put 10 ml of water in the 10-ml graduated cylinder. Pour that into an empty 50-ml cylinder.

3. What is the level of the liquid in the larger cylinder? _____

4. How many times are necessary to pour 10 ml of water into the 50-ml cylinder to exactly reach the 50 ml mark? _____

Soapy Water

1. Put 9 ml of water in the 10-ml graduated cylinder. How many drops of water are necessary to raise the level of water to 10 ml? _____

2. Put 10 ml of water in the 10-ml graduated cylinder. Pour that into an empty 50-ml cylinder.

3. What is the level of the liquid in the larger cylinder? _____

4. How many times are necessary to pour 10 ml of water into the 50-ml cylinder to exactly reach the 50 ml mark? _____

Questions:

1. What is the difference between being precise and being accurate in measuring? Is one more important than the other?

2. What is the number of drops of water per milliliter produced by a standard medicine dropper?

3. What is the meniscus, and how is a graduated cylinder read to take into account the effect of the meniscus?

4. Is there a difference between the rated capacity of a container and the "capacity to the rim"?

SCIENCE LESSONS

Lesson 61

VOLUME OF A MIXTURE: SAND AND WATER

Level: For middle school students (enrichment and problem-solving skills)

Purpose: To gain experience in lab techniques and to develop an understanding of the volume of different substances

Time: About 45 minutes

Materials: For each pair of students:

- Two 100-ml graduated cylinders; two 100-ml beakers
- A quantity of masonry (building) sand and a quantity of sandbox or golf course sand

(For younger students, divide the pairs into two groups. The pairs in one group will measure one kind of sand, and those in the other group will measure the other. The two groups will then compare their data, so each pair will only need one cylinder, one beaker, and one type of sand.)

Procedure:

1. Each pair of students will be given a sufficient supply of the two types of sand. Direct the students to measure out no more than 50 ml of each kind of sand in the graduated cylinder and then put the measured sand into each of the two beakers.

2. Next, students should measure out no more than 50 ml of water into the graduated cylinder, then carefully pour one of the batches of measured sand into the water and agitate gently. They should measure the total amount of sand and water. Then they should repeat these steps with the other cylinder and the remaining measured sand.

3. Students will then use the worksheet to calculate the percentage of sand that is air.

4. Recover the sand and dry it out for use later, but remember that after four to six uses, air percentages in the masonry sand will approach that of what is in the sandbox or golf course sand. The masonry sand has lower percentages of air because so much of the space between the particles of sand is taken up with dirt. Make sure that the students figure that out. Use the example of a room full of balls of different sizes, such as basketballs, soccer balls, baseballs, golf balls, and marbles, compared to a room full of soccer balls. Which would have more air (or which would have less empty space)?

Evaluation: Students will be able to discuss the difference in measuring the volume of pourable solids such as sand and what might affect that volume.

VOLUME OF A MIXTURE: SAND AND WATER Worksheet

Name: _____

Procedure

1. Measure out no more than 50 ml of each kind of sand in one of the 100-ml graduated cylinders. You may use less than 50 ml, but no more than that.

2. Pour that sand into one of the small beakers. Why did we not measure the sand in that beaker to begin with?

3. Measure out no more than 50 ml of water in each of the graduated cylinders and then carefully pour the sand into each of the cylinders.

4. Data:

	Masonry Sand	Sandbox Sand
Volume of sand		
Volume of water		
Calculated volume of sand and water		
Measured volume of sand and water		
Difference between calculated and measured volumes		
Percentage of sand that is air		

Class Averages for percentage of air:

Masonry sand _____

Sandbox sand _____

Questions:

1. What was the volume of the sand particles without the air in each sample?

2. How much of the water that was in the cylinder went to fill up air spaces in the dry sand?

3. What was the volume of the water that was sitting on top of the sand?

4. What percentage of the dry sand that you started with was sand alone?

5. What reason can you give to explain why the two types of sand did not have the same percentage of air in them?

6. How would you measure the volume of just the particles in a sample of sugar?

7. How would you measure the volume of a sponge? What are you actually measuring when you use that method?

8. Would you rather buy jelly beans by the pound or by the pint? Why?

SCIENCE LESSONS

Lesson 62

WHAT COLORS ARE IN YOUR MARKER?

Level: For middle school students (enrichment and incentive activity)

Purpose: To demonstrate the use of chromatography to separate mixtures; to show how characteristic properties can be used to differentiate among substances

Time: About 60 minutes

Materials: For each student or group of students:

- Several strips of chromatography paper, chemical filter paper, or large coffee filters (preferably not the basket variety)
- Two tall thin widemouthed jars or other clear containers
- Hanging clips (which can be made from large paper clips)
- Scissors
- A selection of water-based markers, ink pens, and fountain pen ink

Procedure:

1. Straighten the paper clips and put them over the mouths of the two jars. Fold each side of the clips down to make a square U that will sit across the top of the jar.

2. Use the worksheet to show the students how to cut strips of chromatography or filter paper long enough to fold over the clips at the top of the containers and to reach almost to the bottom. The strips should be narrow enough that they do not touch the sides of the container. The bottom of the strips should be pointed so that just the end will touch the water that will be in the bottom of each container. Do not put the water in the containers yet.

3. Allow the students to select two different markers and to draw a heavy line with the markers across the end of each strip just above the point.

4. Put enough water in the bottom of each container so that it is deep enough to just reach the point of the paper strip.

5. Direct students to gently lower the strips into the containers and suspend the strips in the containers.

6. You can initiate a discussion about why the water is moving up the paper. You can use a capillary tube and colored water to show how colored water moves up the tube as a result of capillary action.

7. When the colors reach most of the way up the strip, have the students remove the strips and place the strips on paper towels to dry. Students should discuss why there are different colors in the markers and whether they expected this and answer questions on the worksheet.

8. While students are doing this, you can do a similar setup with a permanent marker. Use two containers and put water in one and acetone in the other. The point is to show that all substances are soluble if the correct solvent is used.

Evaluation: Students will develop an understanding of mixtures and of how colors are used to create other colors. Students will be able to describe capillary action and how solvents can be used to separate mixtures.

WHAT COLORS ARE IN YOUR MARKER? Worksheet

Name: _____

Directions

1. You will need two containers, two hangers, several strips of paper, scissors, and two markers or pens.

2. Cut the paper into strips that are narrow enough to fit inside the containers without touching the sides and long enough to almost reach the bottom while having a small flap at the top to fold over the hanger. Cut the end of the strip into a point.

3. Draw a thick line with your marker or pen at the bottom of the strip just above the point.

4. Put a small amount of water in the bottom of the container that is just enough to come up to the point of the strip of paper.

5. Gently place the strip into the container with the tip just touching the water.

6. Watch what happens!

7. Take the strip out when the water almost reaches the top and place the strip on a paper towel to dry.

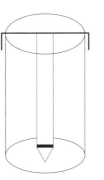

Questions

1. What is the solvent for your ink?

   a. What would happen if you left something written with this ink out in the rain?

2. What happened when the paper came in contact with the water?

3. Did the ink spread out a bit when you initially drew the line on the paper?

4. What happened to the ink as the water moved up the paper?

5. Was your ink a mixture of colors or was it one color?

    a. How did you know that?

6. How did the permanent markers in the demonstration containers differ from the ink that you used?

7. What does this tell you about the dyes used in clothing?

8. Is dry cleaning really dry? How does it differ from washing?

SCIENCE LESSONS

Lesson 63
PENDULUMS

Level: For middle school students and above (enrichment and incentive activity)

Purpose: To investigate the properties of simple pendulums and to determine whether it is weight of the pendulum or length of the suspension that determines how fast the pendulum swings. It is *very* important that you not tell the students what will determine the period of the pendulum; the lab will help them do that. The point of working with experiential learners is that if you give them answers, they lose interest.

Time: About 60 minutes to do the activity; more time to prepare a graph of the data and an analysis (for older students)

Materials:

- Two simple pendulums—various bobs that can be suspended by a length of string or fishing line. The bobs can be weights from a weight set with a hook on the top, fishing sinkers, or the like. Make sure that the bob is heavier than the length of string which suspends it and the bob is fairly compact—don't use pens, for example, as they don't hang straight and it is hard to judge when they have reached the end of their swing. Also two different lengths of string, which can also vary in thickness, can be used.
- Some method to suspend the pendulums that won't wobble. The best is to use a C-clamp to hold a ring stand on a table and a test tube clamp on the ring stand sticking out over the edge of the table. If you don't have that equipment, ask the chemistry teacher.
- A meter stick.
- A stop watch or some method to measure seconds.
- A balance (only need one or two for the whole class).
- Worksheet and graph paper.

Procedure:

1. Set up the device to hold the pendulums. Whatever you use, the important factors are that the pendulum can swing freely and that the device for holding the top does not wobble. Also make sure that top of the suspension is firmly attached, because if it is looped around what is holding it, the loop will move, and that will change the motion of the pendulum.

2. Discuss with the students what they think is going to change the rate at which the pendulums swing. Ask them to think about their experience on playground swings or other similar activities. They should then formulate a hypothesis about which will change the rate at which the pendulum swings—the weight of the bob or the length of the suspension. In this discussion, point out what is involved in determining a round trip for a pendulum; each student should figure out how to decide when his or her pendulum has completed a round trip.

3. Have the students weigh each of their bobs with the suspensions. Once the pendulums are attached, students should measure the length of the pendulum from the point of attachment to the top of the bob.

4. Direct the students to measure the period of each pendulum, filling in the required data on their worksheet.

5. Once all the students have collected their data, have them fill out the table and graph the class data.

Evaluation: Students will be able to discuss the properties of a simple pendulum and will know that it is length of suspension, not weight of bob, that determines the period of a pendulum. Students will be able to collect and graph data and to prepare a report of the exercise.

PENDULUMS Worksheet

Name: _____

1. Physical properties of your pendulums:

Mass of bob	Length of suspension
A. _____	_____
B. _____	_____

2. Period of the pendulum studied

Observations:

Trial No	No. of round trips in 60.0 seconds (or 30.0 sec × 2)	
	A	B
1		
2		
3		
4		
6		
Avg.		

Period = Average number of round trips

Average time in seconds (remember, the average time in seconds should always be 60 seconds)

A = _____cycles/sec

B = _____cycles/sec

3. Collect the data on all of the pendulums used in class using the table on page 205 and (for older students) graph the data.

Questions

1. What is the period of a pendulum?

2. From the data in this lab, one may conclude that the following factors do *not* affect the period of a pendulum.

3. One may conclude that the pendulum's period does depend on:

For advanced students: Collect all of the data from the class and graph the period of the pendulum as a function of its length. From the graph determine if there is a systematic relationship between the two factors.

Name of lab partners	Weight of bob	Length of suspension (cm)	Period of pendulum (cycles/sec)

SCIENCE LESSONS

5

Study Strategies

Jacob came into the science classroom dragging his feet. He was one of the best students, and the teacher was surprised to see him looking so down, as he usually bounced into the classroom ready for science. He reported that he had spent all weekend studying for a test in English and he had just failed it. The science teacher was sure that he hadn't done that badly; he had just gotten a very high mark on a recent test in science class, and told him that it was sometimes hard to tell how well you do on a test. Oh, no, he replied, he had known so little that he had left half of the test blank. "I studied all the wrong things, and I couldn't remember anything about what was asked on the test." The science teacher asked him why he had no trouble on tests in science class; he replied that the material was based on what was done in lab and he could easily remember that. What he had trouble with was paying attention to what he read. The teacher knew that his reading skills were fine so she and Jacob sat down and tried to figure out what was easy and what was hard for him to do. What they came up with is described in the lesson *Study in Bursts* in this chapter; Jacob brought his grades up by two letters in less than a month using this method.

The problem with much of the material on study techniques is the belief that there is one best way to study. That simply isn't true. There isn't even one best way for one person to study, as study skills are dependent on so many different factors. There is not a lot of research examining learning styles and academic success, but some supports the notion that active learners learn best when they can actively engage in a lesson (Sheridan & Steele-Dadzie, 2005). On the other hand, research with graduate students found that females more than males preferred to learn using aural and visual methods, and that neither males nor females preferred reading or kinesthetic approaches (Ramayah, Sivanandan, Nasrijal, Letchumanan, & Leong, 2009). The problem with this study, as with many studies which involve students in tertiary or graduate education, is that the students are successful learners. They have graduated from secondary school and have skills in traditional study methods—reading, listening, and writing. In fact, most of the studies about how students learn involve students who have already graduated from high school.

There isn't a lot of information about how students in elementary and secondary schools learn. Most of the information for these students has an emphasis on teaching in different ways. For example, one teaching approach that varies the substance of what is learned, the methods used to teach, and the outcome of instruction is *differentiated instruction* (Tomlinson, 2004). How the teacher decides to differentiate instruction varies, but generally most will include some hands-on or other active instructional methods. The focus here is on teaching and not on learning. Certainly, good teaching is necessary for students to learn, but they also need to acquire skills which will enable them to begin to acquire information for themselves.

The issue is determining the age at which students are self-aware enough to begin to understand which methods work for them and which do not. In the story above, Jacob was a junior in high school and did not appear to know how he learned. However, when he worked together with his teacher, he easily recognized what approaches for him resulted in successful learning and which did not. He just did not know that he did not have to study the way the teacher told him to, that he could study in a way that was effective for him. In fact, one of his teachers from another subject area came to his science teacher, very concerned that Jacob's new study approach was going to cause him to do even worse than he had already. The concern was that there was no possible way Jacob was going to be able to focus enough to learn the material. The science teacher asked how well Jacob had done on his last quiz; the other teacher admitted that Jacob had a perfect 10 points out of 10, but the teacher was still unconvinced. Only after Jacob raised his grade for the marking period would the teacher admit that the method just might work for this particular student.

The point of the strategies in this section is that there are very effective methods that help students learn that require interaction between the student and the lesson. Just because a student doesn't learn well by reading or listening doesn't mean the student can't learn. Find out what the student does well and then figure out why. Research is clear that many boys do better when they like the course or the teacher (Freudenthaler et al., 2008; Koepke & Harkins, 2008). Boys report that they like classes where there is more activity and where the lessons are more interactive (Reichart & Hawley, 2009). The problem is that boys are less likely to develop new strategies on their own or to ask a fellow student for ideas (Stumpf, 1998).

Good teaching provides students with a myriad of avenues to learn and then points out when that method works: "Why don't you try writing down all of the words and their meanings? That seems to work well for you."

Interactive study methods encourage students to

- write as much as they read,
- find connections among what they are learning, so as to improve memory, and
- get physically involved in reviewing material.

Lesson 64

ACADEMIC FOOTBALL

Level: For middle school students and above (review and alternative modality)

Purpose: It can be hard for the active learner to pay attention during a class review of material. This exercise involves all students, and the competitive element will engage many students.

Time: Probably no longer than 30 to 45 minutes, but once you have done it, you will have a better idea of what suits your students.

Materials:

- Questions from material to be reviewed

Procedure:

1. Students will be divided by the teacher into three groups. Make sure that eventually all students get a chance to take all positions.

2. Two groups will be the teams and one group will be the referees. Each team should have about five or six students on it. If your class is large, you may want to assign some students to be substitutes to be put into a team when someone misses two or three questions.

3. Each team elects a quarterback; that student alone may speak for the team. Any blurting out of answers by other members will be ignored.

4. The referees decide who is going to keep score, who will be the timekeeper, who will ask questions, who will check up on the validity of answers, and who is in charge of fouls.

5. The game begins by tossing a coin and the quarterbacks call heads or tails.

6. The questioner begins by asking a question to the winning team. That question is worth 7 points. If the team misses the question, they lose 7 points. If the team is not sure of the answer, but wishes to try it, they can elect to go for a field goal worth 3 points. They lose 3 points if they are wrong. If they have no idea of the answer, they must punt, and the other team gets an opportunity for a 7-point touchdown or a 3-point field goal. If the original team misses the question, then the other team can try for a field goal.

7. The timekeepers keep track of the time for each quarterback. Once that time has expired, probably 5 or 10 minutes, another student on the team gets a chance at quarterback. Timekeepers also keep track of how long each team is allowed before being required to answer or to punt—probably about 1 minute.

8. The head referee is in charge of monitoring fouls. A student has committed a foul if he makes a derogatory statement about a member of his own team or about a member of the opposite team. The referee should have a yellow

STUDY STRATEGY LESSONS

handkerchief that he can throw down to mark when a foul is committed. If a student commits two fouls, he is benched and a substitute brought in to take his place.

9. This can be a fast-paced game that will engage students and get all involved in getting the right answer.

10. The winning team can be first to go to lunch, or can pick one question on the test not to answer. Since student membership on a team is very fluid, no trophy or visible sign of success will be appropriate.

11. You might even have students bring in questions for this game. Just the act of writing questions is a good review as well.

12. This exercise is written using football as the basis, but you can adapt the game for the sport of the season. This works equally well as Academic Basketball or Academic Baseball.

Evaluation: Student performance on tests will be improved by all students engaging in the review. Even the referees have to pay attention to what is going on, so all students are involved in the review.

Lesson 65

FAMILY TREES or CONCEPT TREES

Level: For middle school students and above (problem-solving skills and alternative modality)

Purpose: Active students may find it difficult to remember all of the individuals in a story or all of the concepts in a chapter. Putting this information in the arrangement of a typical family tree will help the student visualize the information.

Time: Will vary

Materials:

- Study material or story
- Tree chart (or the students can make their own)

Procedure:

1. Once students have identified the material they are working with, they will begin to group the characters or concepts by families or common factors.

2. Highlighters or colored pencils can be used to provide a visual method to group information or individuals. For example, all female names could be written in ink and all male names in pencil; all verbs could be written in ink and all nouns in pencil.

Family tree charts

3. Grouping by families: using *The Adventures of Huckleberry Finn* as an example, on the family tree chart, 1—Huckleberry Finn, 2—family, 3—friends, 4—Pap, 5—adopted family, 6—Tom Sawyer, 7—Jim. 8 and 9 are blank because we don't know anything more about Huck's parents and students should indicate that. 10—Widow Douglas/Miss Watson, 11—Judge Thatcher, 12—Aunt Polly, 13—Silas and Sally Phelps, 14—Jim's wife and children, 15—Miss Watson (to whom Jim belongs). Students can draw lines linking the various characters and writing on the lines what the relationships are.

4. Grouping by areas: Using biology as an example, on the family tree chart, 1—plants with seeds, 2—angiosperms, 3—gymnosperms, 4—monocotyledons, 5—dicotyledons, 6—those with needles, 7—those with leaves. The last row can be used for giving examples of each: 8—bananas, 9—grass, 10—roses, 11—beans, 12—pine trees, 13—yew bushes, 14—ginkgo trees, 15—sago palms.

5. Grouping by meaning: Using the word *share* as an example, 1—share, 2—verb, 3—noun, 4—divide, 5—give information, 6—a section, 7—a part of a company, and the last row can be synonyms for each category: 8—split between, 9—hand some to each, 10—tell the facts, 11—release information, 12—a slice, 13—a piece, 14—stock certificate, 15—a part of the business.

Note

6. You will note that these examples fit the accompanying charts, but sometimes information will not. It will help students to learn to adapt the charts for the information that they are classifying. At the beginning, make sure that the information does fit the chart or adapt the chart to fit the information that students are being required to sort.

Evaluation: Students will find it easier to remember material because they are learning each fact in context with the rest of related information and writing the information gives them a physical activity keeping their attention on the task at hand.

FAMILY TREE CHART

Name: _____

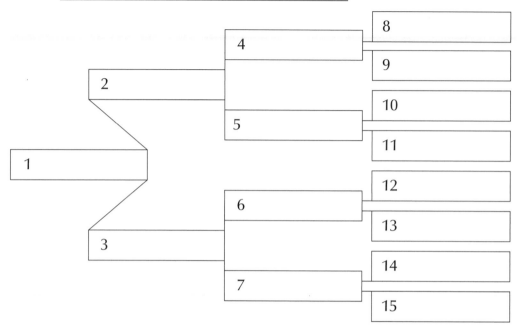

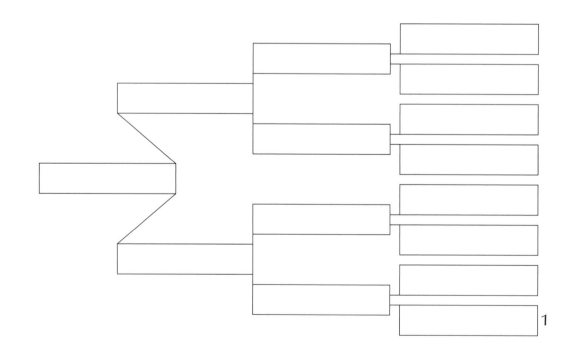

Lesson 66

FOLDING VOCAB

Level: For middle school students and above (review; this technique can be used in a wide variety of subjects)

Purpose: Experiential learners frequently have trouble learning material if all they do is just look at it. Writing information several times is one of the best ways to learn anything, but without a structured method, many students will not attempt that way. This strategy gives students something concrete to do to learn vocabulary. Flash cards do not work as well as this method.

Time: This is probably something for students to do as part of homework.

Materials:

- List of vocabulary words
- Lined notebook paper

Procedure:

1. Students will get their list of words together with the meaning of the words.

2. They will write the words in the notebook paper on the far left of the red vertical line. If the paper is punched, they will have to work around the holes in this area.

3. They will then write the meaning of the words on the same line to the right of the red vertical line.

4. Then they fold the paper lengthwise like a book, so that the written side is now inside the folded paper.

5. The second vertical fold goes the other way, so that the list of words is exposed but the meanings are covered by the folded paper. (See the picture.)

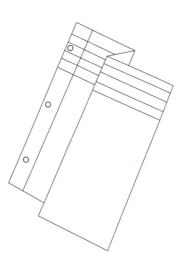

6. The students can now see the words, and have a clean sheet of paper on which to write the meaning. Once they have done so, they can pull the paper straight and will see the correct meaning and what they just wrote on the same side of the paper.

7. If students are very careful and write small, they can make this fold twice. Otherwise, they can just bring the far right edge of the paper to the vertical line, covering all the meanings and just exposing the words.

Evaluation: Students can turn in their folded vocabulary sheets for checking, but the real test of whether or not this works will be on a test.

Lesson 67

INTERACTIVE NOTEBOOKS

Level: Can be adapted for all levels (incentive activity and alternative modality)

Purpose: Experiential learners do better when they have something to experience or to do. Interactive notebooks provide a means for active learners to use their kinesthetic and iconic skills to supply organization for more verbal lessons. The notebook will also provide structure for the students to organize the information from class.

Time: This will vary among students, but it can be a part of homework or it can be an activity to do in class.

Materials:

- Notebook—preferably ring-bound, with dividers of various varieties and notebook paper. If students are to have a different notebook for each course, please remember that creates a lot for a student to carry so 1-inch notebooks will probably be sufficient.
- Magazines; colored pencils and markers; glue; tape; scissors.

Procedure:

1. Students should set up their notebooks according to teacher directions. The dividers may be used to separate homework, handouts, and various topics.

2. *Everything* goes into the notebook. If the class is given handouts, make sure that they are punched correctly, so that the students can put the handout immediately into the notebook. One section can provide a place for students to write down homework assignments. Some dividers are actually pockets; those can be used to store homework to turn in.

3. If you want students to take notes in class, have a section for that purpose. If you want students to keep track of homework and long-term assignments, you can give students calendar pages for the front of the notebook with blocks to write in the assignments. This will also provide a place for students to learn how to divide a long-term assignment into shorter and smaller blocks, putting those short-term goals on the calendar.

4. The *left* side of the page is for teacher input: notes provided by teachers, content, mini-lessons, examples of work, and so forth. The *right* side of the page is for student input in which they take the information and *do* something with it: for instance, provide examples or paste in pictures which are illustrative of the lesson.

5. Examples:

    a. *Grammar lesson:* The *left* side of the page is supplied by the teacher and contains notes on prepositional phrases, what they are, how they are constructed, what are the parts, and so forth. Also on that page is a picture from a magazine of something—for this lesson it really doesn't matter what the picture was. In class, the teacher and the student list all of the prepositional phrases evident in the picture such as: *the model is beside the car, the car is atop the road, the road is along the ditch,* and the like. Then on the *right* side, students find or create their own images or pictures and list at least 20 prepositional phrases to describe the image.

b. *Math lesson:* The *left* side of the page is supplied by the teacher and contains notes on order of operations. In extremely large letters at the top of the page is the acronym PEMDAS (**p**arenthesis, **e**xponents, **m**ultiplication, **d**ivision, **a**ddition, **s**ubtraction). For each of the terms, the teacher supplies a description of what that term means and gives an example of it. At the bottom of the page are some exercises which the class does together, such as those in the PEMDAS exercise in the math section of this workbook. On the *right* side, students make their own problems, working them correctly as well as incorrectly, showing the difference in answers between following the rules and not following the rules. They then make up a scenario where correctly following the order of operation makes a difference in the amount of money something costs.

c. *Civics lesson:* The *left* side of the page is a copy of several ads for individuals running for a local judgeship, together with a description of the duties of the judge. (These should not be for an actual election in the area where the school is located.) Students list the qualifications of the individuals, matching them with the duties of the judge. On the *right* side of the page, students are to list the duties of the president of the student government in their school and then develop a campaign poster for a fictional person running for that position, showing how to get the information across accurately.

d. *Life sciences lesson:* The *left* side of the page contains notes from the teacher on photosynthesis together with a diagram of the chemistry of what happens when green plants turn carbon dioxide and water into sugar and oxygen. On the *right* side of the page, students are to find examples in the newspaper or in magazines of businesses that are trying to improve the balance of carbon dioxide and oxygen in the world by planting trees, lowering the carbon footprint, driving cars with lower carbon emissions, and the like.

Evaluation: This provides a place for all student work to be compiled, resulting in a portfolio of all the work the student has done. This enables students to practice organizational skills and to give them practice in producing work.

Lesson 68

MUSICAL REVIEW CHAIRS

Level: Can be adapted for all levels (review: in all courses)

Purpose: Provide a structure for review while allowing students the chance to move around the room. Many active learners find it easy to learn when music is playing, and this will give those students an opportunity to practice math while listening to music.

Time: About 35 to 40 minutes

Materials:

- Popular music and a CD player or computer (Earlier in the week, the prize for doing well on an exercise can be to pick the music for this exercise)
- Clipboards for every student (optional)
- Index cards with math problems. (Just copy a worksheet, cut into strips, and glue to the index cards. You just saved lots of paper!) You can also use questions from a textbook or any questions that elicit a written answer from the students
- Answer key for checking
- Alternate assignment, such as homework

Procedure: Student chairs are placed in a circle. Math problems or other questions on index cards are placed on desktops. Every fourth desk is a "catch-up" desk, with no index card on that desk. The teacher plays popular music as students begin working on their problems or questions. When the music stops, the students move to the next seat and start on a new problem. At the catch-up desk, the students may finish uncompleted problems or begin on an alternate assignment that they have on their clipboard. The students continue moving around the circle until all problems are copied.

1. Explain the purpose of Musical Review Chairs.
2. Students need paper, pencils, clipboard, and an alternate assignment. They will clean off desks and arrange chairs.
3. Place index cards on desks, leaving every fourth desk blank.
4. Start the music, then stop it after 1 to 2 minutes. Students rotate.
5. The round continues until the first student returns to original desk.
6. Students can stay at the desk and check answers. Some students may need a few more minutes to complete the assignment before you check the work.

When to use

Musical Review Chairs is a good review activity. This works well 1 or 2 days before a test.

Evaluation: Musical Review Chairs is a structured activity that gives students a chance to practice skills in a rhythmic, seated activity that allows for movement. The extra seat provides time to catch up on unfinished problems. The teacher directs the movement and manages the music from one place. Limiting the amount of time at each station helps students develop recall and problem-solving skills. The prize for the most correct answers can be to pick the music for the next time.

Lesson 69
STUDY IN BURSTS

Level: For middle school students and above (alternative modality and incentive activity)

Purpose: Many active learners waste an incredible amount of time when they are studying as they cannot focus for long on a reading assignment or other passive homework. This strategy will not work for all students, but for those for whom it does work, it can be a lifesaver.

Time: No longer than 2 hours at a time

Materials:

- Homework
- Long table or several different places to work in one room
- A kitchen timer (if necessary)

Procedure:

1. The student gathers all of his or her homework together with the books, worksheets, papers, or the materials that are required to complete all of the work.

2. The student places each assignment in its own pile and jots down what is to be done on a sticky note, which he places on the top.

3. The student rates the assignments from most passive to most active—passive homework would require only reading, while active homework would involve writing or solving problems. The student assigns a number to each homework assignment, with 1 being the most passive. The highest number will depend upon the number of assignments the student has.

4. The student puts the piles of homework on the long table or around the room so that the homework is arranged with a passive assignment first, then an active one, then passive, then active. For example, if there are five assignments the numbers would be 1, 5, 2, 4, 3.

5. The student begins the most passive assignment, which is likely to be reading. It is common that active learners find it difficult to read for any length of time while continuing to focus on the material, so the following techniques are designed to lengthen the amount of material this student can focus on at one time. For a textbook:

   a. The first step is to look at the table of contents for the chapter. The student should notice what the topic is and make some prediction about what he will find in the chapter. The student should talk out loud to himself about this: "So this chapter is going to be about the beginning of the Revolutionary War. It looks like we will cover some stuff about taxes—oh, yeah, I remember—taxation without representation—I guess that will be in here." Talking out loud requires more concentration than just reading the material, and it helps students to focus.

   b. If the student is helped by walking around the room while he reads, he should pick up the book and read.

   c. Then the student should begin to read the material. The student should note the important points by highlighting, writing notes in the margin, or writing notes on a sticky note which can be placed over the paragraph. (If the school owns the book, the student may not be allowed to mark in the book.) One problem that some students have is that they tend to underline or highlight most of a chapter. The result is that it is difficult for them to use the chapter for review, as most of the material has been noted. These students tend to highlight examples or supporting material because that information is easier to visualize. What they need to do is discuss the material in the chapter with themselves to determine what word or phrase the examples or supporting material refer to. That is the concept and the only material that gets noted. With less material noted, the student can use the book as a review tool. You may need to help your students learn to pick out the concept. Make it a game and give points to the student who can find the correct word or phrase.

   For a story or other reading assignments, a student should stop every page or so and talk to himself about what is going on in the story. "It looks as if Johnny is going to get into trouble here because he is doing what he was told not to do."

6. Once the student can no longer focus on the passive assignment (even if that is only 3 minutes), the student switches to an active assignment such as working math problems. However, the student is only to do a portion of this homework either working for 5 to 10 minutes or doing one fourth of the assigned problems.

7. When the student has reached the time limit or completed the problem set, the student moves to another passive homework.

8. When the student can no longer focus on that passive homework, the student moves on to another active assignment for a limited period of time or portion of the assignment.

9. Eventually, the student will return to the beginning and pick up the passive homework where he left off. Before doing so, the student should either glance at the material already covered or try to remember what was read before. This provides constant review, which will result in better memory for the material.

10. The concern from teachers is that the student will not complete the assignment or will find it difficult to focus on the reading. The student is already having trouble with that, and if, while reading, he pays attention only 20 percent of the time, the student is wasting 80 percent of the time available to study. That time can be used more effectively.

11. Chewing gum has been shown to help memory (Wilkinson, Scholey, & Wesnes, 2002), and it can help the active learner to chew gum while studying. More recent research casts some doubt about the memory effect of chewing gum, but does support the notion that gum chewing helps increase alertness (Smith, 2009).

Evaluation: The student should report being better able to complete more homework assignments, which should be reflected in better assignments and test results.

Lesson 70
WWWWWH (Who, What, When, Where, Why, How)

Level: For middle school students and above (review and problem-solving skills)

Purpose: Experiential learners can have a hard time focusing on passive activities such as reading. Giving them something to do while they are reading helps keep their focus on the material and they will not daydream as much.

Time: This will vary among students, but it can be a part of homework or it can be an activity to do in class.

Materials:

- A reading assignment
- A WWWWWH worksheet

Procedure:

1. Students will have a WWWWWH worksheet for each reading assignment. If the assignment is part of a continuing story, such as that from a novel or collection of stories, the sheets should be clipped together, but students should not just continue to work on the new assignment on the old sheet.

2. As students read, they will list individuals under the first *W* (*Who*) on the sheet beside the numbers in the order of appearance. If several individuals appear together in a subsequent *W* (for example, if two characters go together to do something), the numbers for both individuals are placed below the appropriate heading—*What, Where, When, Why,* or *How* headings. That is why the only numbers on the sheet are under the section for *Who*, and there are blanks in the other sections for students to number appropriately. When looking at a description, the number in front will identify the individuals involved.

3. If this technique is used with material other than a story, the list of those listed in the Who section may include nations, political parties, groups, techniques, or any person or approach which acts or influences others.

Evaluation: This provides a scaffold for students to take notes in such a way that the notes can be easily connected and linked. Memory is enhanced through elaboration; simply knowing that someone did something may not be enough for a student to remember a fact. The evaluation of this strategy is an increase in student recall of information from a written source.

WWWWWH Worksheet

Name: _____

Fill in the following information. Those listed in the first section get numbered in order of appearance. If there are too many for this sheet, use another one. In the following sections, briefly describe for each individual, what happens, where it happens, when it happens, why it happens (if you know), and how it happens. In the blanks, put the appropriate numbers of those listed in the Who section who are involved in the events described on the rest of the sheet. If several individuals are involved in the same event, put all the numbers in front of that event.

WHO

1.   4.

2.   5.

3.   6.

WHAT

_____

_____

_____

_____

WHERE

_____

_____

_____

_____

WHEN

_____

_____

_____

WHY

_____

_____

_____

HOW

_____

_____

_____

Lesson 71

MAYDAY

(In French class, you can title this *M'aidez*, which translates to "help me.")

Level: For all levels (problem-solving skills and review)

Purpose: It can be difficult to get students to pay attention to what you say in class, and trying to get them to pay attention to what other students are saying can be even more difficult. Every teacher has had to answer the same question multiple times when students don't realize that another student has asked the same question.

Procedure:

1. If a student is asked a question and either cannot give an answer or gives a wrong answer, the student may call on another student to provide some assistance—make a "Mayday" call. That student may not answer for the first student, but may provide essential information or hints to help the first student answer the question. If the supplied help is incorrect or does not result in a correct answer, the student will call on another student. If that doesn't result in a correct answer, the teacher will then provide assistance.

2. A variation on this is after a student has supplied an answer, the teacher turns to another student and say, "What do you think about this answer? Do you agree or disagree?" At the beginning, the first student will make some comment about his answer being wrong, but you should tell the class that you have not passed on whether or not the original answer is correct, and you want the class to learn to listen to each other and to think critically about what is said in class.

Evaluation:

1. In the version where a student calls on another for help, if the help results in a successful answer, both students receive points. If the help is correct, but does not result in a successful answer, the questioner loses a point and the helper gains a point. If the helper gives incorrect help and the questioner still cannot answer, the helper loses a point, and the questioner neither gains nor loses a point. If the questioner is helped by the suggestions, both students get a point.

2. The grading for "What do you think about this answer?" is similar to the first version. However, if the second student does not agree with the first, call on a third student to supply an answer or comment. Even if two students agree, that may not be the correct answer. If not, have the students who are answering get together to see if they can come up with the correct answer when they work together.

Lesson 72
STANDING AT BOARDS

Level: For all levels (alternative modality)

Purpose: Standing at boards is a semiphysical activity that gives active learners a focused, interactive way to complete practice work and discuss mathematical processes. Students work in a structured, planned way and are able to use their individual strengths to complete tasks beside a partner or alone. This strategy keeps them awake and prevents the doodling and calculator games that occur when students are seated with paper and pencil skill work. They get immediate feedback and are rewarded for effort in front of peers. It eliminates the "hovering" posture of the teacher when leaning over students. The teacher becomes a "shoulder-to-shoulder" partner in the classroom.

Time: Variable, but at least 20 minutes

Materials:

- Whiteboards or chalkboards around the room, or medium-sized whiteboards which can be propped up against the walls
- Markers or chalk; erasers or socks; pencil and paper to record points or answers
- Student assignment on clipboards (optional)

Procedure: Standing at Boards was designed as a strategy to enable active learners to complete mathematical tasks. However, any questions which involve steps can also be used in this activity, such as drawing body systems or diagramming a sentence. Use this strategy for practice, review, or problem solving. Students discuss procedures and make comments about mistakes. The teacher will help the students make the connection that each has different academic strengths and that the "shoulder-to-shoulder" strategy will be used in the future jobs and in sports to achieve their goals.

If there is not ample board space for all students to stand at once, allow students to work as partners, one seated and one standing. Have them switch roles after every third problem. The seated partner can read the problems to the standing partner and can serve as an assistant in problem solving.

1. Give students the assignments and point values for each problem.

2. Students go to the boards to complete tasks.

3. In a very effective test review session, the teacher stands and calls out "quick" problems for student to write and solve. (Students can tally correct responses above their work.)

4. In efficient practice or problem solving-sessions, the teacher walks around the room, checks for accuracy, helps individual or pairs correct their errors, and takes advantages of the "teachable moment" when a classic math error or "perfect" procedure is shown in student work. (Teacher initials and records the points on student sheet.)

5. Students may explain their work to the whole class.

6. Student points are recorded or collected.

Evaluation: This lesson is for review. Student progress and focus on task will be the best evaluation of this strategy.

Lesson 73
STANDING TO LEARN

Level: For all levels (alternative modality and review)

Purpose: Teachers have noted that many active learners find it difficult to pay attention in class. This attentional issue is not caused by any learning disability; it is just that these students have a lot of energy and sitting in class does not use enough of their energy. Anything that will help them focus and use some energy at the same time will help keep them on track and improve the class environment as well.

Procedure:

1. *Supplying answers:* No one stands in class unless the teacher gives permission or requests that the student stand. When the teacher wishes to ask a question, she will pick a student and say something like, "Mr. Smith, please stand for the next question." The student stands, and the teacher asks the question after the student is fully on his feet. The advantage here is that it gives the student time to get prepared to listen to a question and to supply an answer. The student will be paying attention and the teacher does not have to repeat the question. We call elementary age children by their first names, but starting in middle school we refer to all of our students as either Mr. Lastname or Miss Lastname. The idea is that standing to answer questions is very formal, and using last names emphasizes the formality. We think you will find that your students will like this approach.

2. *Asking questions:* If a student needs to ask a question in class, she will raise her hand. Once the teacher calls on the student, she is allowed to stand and ask her question. The advantage here is that the student has the full attention of the teacher and you reduce some off-task questions such as "What's for lunch?"

3. *Class control:* If a student blurts out an answer, he is ignored, or the teacher will say something like "You have not been invited to stand, and until you are, please be quiet." You are likely to find that students will police this themselves, reminding the offenders that they are not on their feet and cannot talk. Learning self-control is a valuable lesson, and this technique helps students develop the ability to wait for questions and answers.

4. *Variations:* Some classes have made a game of this. For example, when declining verbs in a foreign language, students can stand rapidly in sequence in the class, standing by rows or columns. As soon as a student stands, he says the next part of speech and then just as rapidly sits down, to be followed by the next student in line. This can look a little like a lot of jack-in-the-boxes, but the students do get exercise, and the faster they go, the more they must pay attention.

Evaluation: If you implement this class control measure, you should find that your class is a bit quieter, partially because only those standing may talk and partially because they are getting a bit of exercise. You should find that you do not have to repeat questions because you don't ask them until the student is standing. Standing in front of people is one of the most prevalent phobias, and this approach will give students a safe place to practice this skill.

Conclusion

All of these lessons, activities, approaches, and techniques have been used by us in our classes. We hope they work for you as well as they have for us. We have asked friends who have never seen the lessons to read them and try them out in order to make sure that the directions and explanations make sense. However, it can sometimes be difficult to phrase directions so that everyone understands them. If you have trouble, do not hesitate to contact me at ajames@anj-online.com for further explanations.

The important point for all of the lessons in this workbook is that they require the student to be actively involved. If too much time is spent explaining the lesson, it will not work the way it was designed. The problem for most experiential learners is that they don't learn from lectures; the more the teacher explains, the less they retain. What works for these students is physical connection to the lesson. After they have experienced the lesson, questions about what they learned will help them connect what happened with the concept. What we frequently hear from teachers is, "But I have to explain what they are to do; otherwise they don't understand and can't learn." In fact, experiential learners don't learn from lectures and do much better with a few pointers and trial-and-error. It may not seem very efficient, but it is their way.

All of these lessons were developed by the authors or by the three teachers we cited in the acknowledgement section. If they seem similar to ones you developed or have seen in other places, it just means that we had similar solutions to similar classroom challenges. We hope that using some of these lessons will provide a trigger for you to start developing some experiential lessons for your classes. Your students will be more engaged in the lesson as a result.

References

Allen, J. (2000). *Yellow brick roads: Shared and guided paths to independent reading 4–12*. Portland, ME: Stenhouse Publishers.

Bednarek, D., Tarnowski, A., & Grabowska, A. (2006). Latencies of stimulus-driven eye movements are shorter in dyslexic subjects. *Brain and Cognition, 60*, 64–69.

Boatella-Costa, E., Costas-Moragas, C., Mussons-Botet, F., Fornieles-Deu, A., & De Cáceres-Zurita, M. L. (2007). Behavioral gender differences in the neonatal period according to the Brazelton scale. *Early Human Development, 83*, 91–97.

Caplan, J. B., & Caplan, P. J. (2005). The perseverative search for sex differences in mathematics ability. In A. M. Gallagher & J. C. Kaufman (Eds.), *Gender differences in mathematics: An integrative psychological approach*. New York: Cambridge University Press.

Cassidy, J. W., & Ditty, K. M. (2001). Gender differences among newborns on a transient otoacoustic emissions test for hearing. *Journal of Music Therapy, 38*(1), 28–35.

Ding, N., & Harskamp, E. (2006). How partner gender influences female students' problem solving in physics education. *Journal of Science Education and Technology, 15*(5), 331–343.

Forbes, E. (1943/1971). *Johnny Tremain*. New York: Houghton Mifflin.

Freudenthaler, H. H., Spinath, B., & Neubauer, A. C. (2008). Predicting school achievement in boys and girls. *European Journal of Personality, 22*, 231–245.

Frome, P. M., & Eccles, J. S. (1998). Parents' influence on children's academic-related perceptions. *Journal of Personality and Social Psychology, 74*(2), 435–452.

Geary, D. C. (2000). Mathematical disorders: An overview for educators. *Perspectives, 26*(3), 6–9.

Geist, E. A., & King, M. (2008). Different, not better: Gender differences in mathematics learning and achievement. *Journal of Instructional Psychology, 35*(1), 43–52.

Giedd, J. N., Blumenthal, J., Jeffries, N. O., Castellanos, F. X., Liu, H., Zijdenbos, A., et al. (1999). Brain development during childhood and adolescence: A longitudinal MRI study. *Nature Neuroscience, 2*(10), 861–863.

Giedd, J. N., Castellanos, F. X., Rajapakse, J. C., Vaituzis, A. C., & Raporport, J. L. (1997). Sexual dimorphism of the developing human brain. *Progress in Neuro-Psychopharmacology & Biological Psychiatry, 21*, 1185–1201.

Goldstein, J. M., Jerram, M., Poldrak, R., Anagnoson, R., Breiter, H. C., Makris, N., et al. (2007). Sex differences in prefrontal cortical brain activity during fMRI of auditory verbal working memory. *Neuropsychology, 19*(4), 509–519.

Graham, S., Berninger, V., Weintraub, N., & Schafer, W. (1998). Development of handwriting speed and legibility in grades 1–9. *The Journal of Educational Research, 92*(1), 42–52.

Graham, S., Harris, K., & Fink, B. (2000). Is handwriting causally related to learning to write? Treatment of handwriting problems in beginning writers. *Journal of Educational Psychology, 92*(4), 620–633.

Halpern, D. F. (2000). *Sex differences in cognitive abilities* (3rd ed.). Mahwah, NJ: Lawrence Erlbaum Associates, Publishers.

Halpern, D. F. (2004). A cognitive-process taxonomy for sex differences in cognitive abilities. *Current Directions in Psychological Science, 13*(4), 135–139.

Huguet, P., & Régner, I. (2007). Stereotype threat among schoolgirls in quasi-ordinary classroom circumstances. *Journal of Educational Psychology, 99*(3), 545–560.

Inzlicht, M., & Ben-Zeev, T. (2003). Do high-achieving female students underperform in private? The implications of threatening environments on intellectual processing. *Journal of Educational Psychology, 95*(4), 796–805.

Jacobs, J. E., & Bleeker, M. M. (2004). Girls' and boys' developing interests in math and science: Do parents matter? *New Directions for Child and Adolescent Development, 106*, 5–21.

James, A. N. (2007). *Teaching the male brain: How boys think, feel, and learn in school.* Thousand Oaks, CA: Corwin.

James, A. N. (2009). *Teaching the female brain: How girls learn math and science.* Thousand Oaks, CA: Corwin.

Johns, M., Schmader, T., & Martens, A. (2005). Knowing is half the battle: Teaching stereotype threat as a means of improving women's math performance. *Psychological Science, 16*(3), 175–179.

Joseph, H. S. S. L., Liversedge, S. P., Blythe, H. I., White, S. J., Gathercole, S. E., & Rayner, K. (2008). Children's and adult's processing of anomaly and implausibility during reading: Evidence from eye movements. *The Quarterly Journal of Experimental Psychology, 61*(5), 708–723.

Kanevsky, L., & Keighley, T. (2003). To produce or not to produce? Understanding boredom and the honor in underachievement. *Roeper Review, 26*(1), 20–28.

Kimura, D. (2000). *Sex and cognition.* Cambridge, MA: A Bradford Book/The MIT Press.

Kimura, D. (2004). Human sex differences in cognition, fact, not predicament. *Sexualities, Evolution & Gender, 6*(1), 45–53.

Koepke, M. F., & Harkins, D. A. (2008). Conflict in the classroom: Gender differences in the teacher-child relationship. *Early Education and Development, 19*(6), 843–864.

Kurtz-Costes, B., Rowley, S. J., Harris-Britt, A., & Woods, T. A. (2008). Gender stereotypes about mathematics and science and self-perceptions of ability in late childhood and early adolescence. *Merrill-Palmer Quarterly, 54*(3), 386–409.

McFadden, D. (1998). Sex differences in the auditory system. *Developmental Neuropsychology, 14*(2/3), 261–298.

Merriam-Webster online dictionary. Retrieved from http://www.merriam-webster.com/dictionary.

Medwell, J., & Wray, D. (2008). Handwriting—a forgotten language skill? *Language and Education: An International Journal, 22*(1), 34–47.

Montgomery, D. (2008). Cohort analysis of writing in year 7 following two, four, and seven years of the National Literacy Strategy. *Support for Learning, 23*(1), 3–11.

Morisset, C. E., Barnard, K. E., & Booth, C. L. (1995). Toddlers' language development: Sex differences within social risk. *Developmental Psychology, 31*(5), 851–865.

National Center for Education Statistics (NCES). (2009). *The nation's report card: An introduction to the National Assessment of Educational Progress (NAEP).* Washington, DC: U.S. Department of Education.

Ramayah, M., Sivanandan, P., Nasrijal, N. H., Letchumanan, T., & Leong, L. C. (2009). Preferred learning style: Gender influence on preferred learning style among business students. *Journal of US-China Public Administration, 6*(4), 65–78.

Rapport, M. D., Bolden, J., Kofler, M. J., Sarver, D. E., Raiker, J. S., & Alderson, R. M. (2009). Hyperactivity in boys with attention-deficit/hyperactivity disorder (ADHD): A ubiquitous core symptom or manifestation of working memory deficits? *Journal of Abnormal Child Psychology, 37*(4), 521–534.

Reichart, M., & Hawley, R. (2009). *Teaching boys: A global study of effective teaching practices.* Toronto, Canada: International Boys' Schools Coalition.

Sandburg, C. (1953). *Abe Lincoln grows up.* Orlando, FL: Harcourt Brace. (Original work published 1926)

Schmithorst, V. J., Holland, S. K., & Dardzinski, B. J. (2008). Developmental differences in white matter architecture between boys and girls. *Human Brain Mapping, 29,* 696–710.

Shalev, R. S. (2004). Developmental dyscalculia. *Journal of Child Neurology, 19*(10), 765–770.

Sheridan, M. J., & Steele-Dadzie, T. E. (2005). Structure of intellect and learning style of incarcerated youth assessment: A means to providing a continuum of educational service in juvenile justice. *The Journal of Correctional Education, 56*(4), 347–371.

Shucard, J. L., & Shucard, D. W. (1990). Auditory evoked potentials and hand preference in 6-month-old infants: Possible gender-related differences in cerebral organization. *Developmental Psychology, 26*(6), 923–930.

Smith, A. (2009). Effects of chewing gum on mood, learning, memory and performance of an intelligence test. *Nutritional Neuroscience, 12* (2), 81–88.

Sokal, L., Katz, H., Chaszewski, L., & Wojcik, C. (2007). Good-bye, Mr. Chips: Male teacher shortages and boys' reading achievement. *Sex Roles, 56,* 651–659.

Spencer, S. J., Steele, C. M., & Quinn, D. M. (1999). Stereotype threat and women's math performance. *Journal of Experimental Social Psychology, 35*(1), 4–28.

Stenström, C., & Ingvarsson, L. (1997). Otitis-prone children and controls: A study of possible predisposing factors. *Acta Oto-Laryngologcia, 117*(1), 87–93.

Stumpf, H. (1998). Gender-related differences in academically talented students' scores and use of time on tests of spatial ability. *Gifted Child Quarterly, 42*(3), 157–171.

Sullivan, A. (2009). Academic self-concept, gender and single-sex schooling. *British Educational Research Journal, 35*(2), 259–288.

Swalander, L., & Taube, K. (2007). Influences of family based prerequisites, reading attitude, and self-regulation on reading ability. *Contemporary Educational Psychology, 32,* 206–230.

Tomlinson, C. A. (2004). *How to differentiate instruction in mixed-ability classrooms* (2nd ed.). Alexandria, VA: Association for Supervision and Curriculum Development.

U.K. Department for Education (2009). *National Curriculum assessments at Key Stage 2 in England, 2009.* Retrieved from http://www.dcsf.gov.uk/rsgateway/DB/SFR/s000865/SFR192009.pdf.

U.S. Department of Education Institute of Education Sciences National Center for Education Statistics (2008). *Digest of education statistics* (2008). Retrieved from http://nces.ed.gov/programs/digest/d08.

Vallance, R. (2002). *Empirical study of a boys' school and boys' motivation.* Paper presented at the Australian Association for Research in Education, Brisbane.

Vande Gaer, E., Pustjens, H., Van Damme, J., & De Munter, A. (2007). Impact of attitudes of peers on language achievement: gender differences. *Journal of Educational Research, 101*(2), 78–92.

Velle, W. (1987). Sex differences in sensory functions. *Perspectives in Biology and Medicine, 30*(4), 490–522.

Wadlington, E., & Wadlington, P. L. (2008). Helping students with mathematical disabilities to succeed. *Preventing School Failure, 53*(1), 2–7.

Wehrwein, E. A., Lujan, H. L., & DiCarlo, S. E. (2006). Gender differences in learning style preferences among undergraduate physiology students. *Advances in Physiology Education, 31*(2), 153–157.

Whitehead, J. M. (2006). Starting school—why girls are already ahead of boys. *Teacher Development, 10*(2), 249–270.

Wilkinson, L., Scholey, A., & Wesnes, K. (2002). Chewing gum selectively improves aspects of memory in healthy volunteers. *Appetite, 38,* 235–236.

Yurglen-Todd, D. A., Killgore, W. D. S., & Cintron, C. B. (2003). Cognitive correlates of medial temporal lobe development across adolescence: A magnetic resonance imaging study. *Perceptual and Motor Skills, 96,* 3–17.